Lifting the Lid

Lifting the Lid

A Guide to Investigative Research

David Northmore

CASSELL

Cassell
Wellington House
125 Strand
London
WC2R 0BB

215 Park Avenue South
New York
NY 10003

First published 1996

British Library Cataloguing-in-Publication Data
A catalogue record for this book is available from the British Library.

Library of Congress Cataloging-in-Publication Data
Northmore, David.
   Lifting the Lid: A Guide to Investigative Research/David
   Northmore.
      p. cm.
Includes bibliographical references and index.
   ISBN (invalid) 0-304-33101-0. — ISBN 0–304–33113–9 (pbk.)
1. Investigative reporting. 2. Research—Methodology. I. Title.
   PN4781.N67 1996
070.4'3—dc20   95–32339 CIP

ISBN 0-304-33109-0 (hardback)
      0-304-33113-9 (paperback)

Typeset by York House Typographic Ltd

Printed and bound in Great Britain by Biddles Ltd, Guildford and King's
Lynn

Contents

Introduction

IN the early autumn of 1993 some 500 student journalists elbowed their way into a university auditorium to hear a panel discussion on investigative journalism being addressed by several leading practitioners in the field.

One of the distinguished panellists asked how many of those present intended to become investigative reporters; more than 300 students raised their hands. The chances are that those aspiring student journalists will fulfil their ambition, for this seminar was taking place in the USA at the University of Missouri's prestigious School of Journalism, which is also the home of Investigative Reporters and Editors Incorporated – a widely respected educational charity with a membership of more than 1,500 working journalists, editors and lecturers.

Investigative journalism is a vibrant industry in the United States, functioning in all branches of the media and at all levels; in the Britain of the 1990s it is a dying craft with a diminishing number of practitioners servicing even fewer outlets. The disturbing truth is that there is not one training course on investigative journalism in the UK – apart from the occasional *ad hoc* lecture or seminar. Even more disturbing is the fact that there is no periodical dedicated to promoting the subject, nor even a training handbook that sets out the basic skills for the ambitious investigative researcher aiming to practise in this country.

Until now, that is. This book has the distinction of being the first published in the United Kingdom on the subject of investigative research and journalism. Hopefully it will not be the last, as it is intended to be part of a broad campaign to encourage a new generation of journalists in a resurgence of campaigning and investigative journalism. However, the skills and tactics of investigative journalism will by no means be of interest only to journalists and others working in the media. There is a wide range of individuals and groups in our society who have a legitimate right – and often a compelling need – to undertake investigative research and to publish the results: political activists, trade unionists, lawyers, members of pressure groups, councillors, academics, librarians and others.

Although this book is primarily aimed at the working journalist, it is also relevant to this broader readership. Therefore, wherever the term 'journalist' appears in the text, read 'journalist or other investigative researcher'. In terms of research there is little that the working journalist is able to do that can not also be done by any other determined and motivated individual.

And one of the key myths of investigative research and journalism that this book seeks to demolish is that this is a prohibitively expensive activity. Not so. As we will find out by exploring the various examples of investigation in each of the following chapters, success in investigative research and journalism owes more to an attitude of mind, combined with a little cunning, than to the application of vast resources.

And although this book has been written from a British point of view, it is not intended to be confined to a British readership. Many of the strategies, tactics, and techniques detailed here can be applied to other developed societies, particularly those that have an historical link with this country and whose economies, political institutions and legal systems are largely or closely modelled on the British system.

The British method of government is, however, the most secretive in the developed world. Many of the official bodies and organizations that wield power in the United Kingdom have their origins in the medieval era, and are not structured or operated with any regard to public scrutiny or democratic accountability. After all, this country still has a constitutional monarchy, an unelected and largely hereditary upper house of parliament and a multi-hierarchical honours system. This is evidence that the values of democracy and meritocracy still struggle for recognition even in the run-up to the twenty-first century.

However, the level and extent of official secrecy in British society has been well documented in recent years. The *Spycatcher* affair, the *Zircon* case, the *Death on the Rock* fiasco and the many other manifestations of official secrecy have been endlessly published, broadcast and debated. In fact, the late 1980s and early 1990s provided a mass of evidence of the damaging and often devastating effects of a system of government that conducts so much official business behind closed doors. The epitome of that evidence has to be the Scott inquiry into the British government's arms-to-Iraq policy which surfaced following the collapse in 1992 of the Old Bailey trial of the three directors of the Matrix Churchill company (a case that we shall be examining from a research point of view in more detail later in this book). According to evidence submitted by government. ministers, former ministers and at least one former prime minister, the British government and civil service were clueless about the activities of the arms industry, and even of the arms procurement sections within government departments.

Further evidence of the adverse effects of this secretive approach came in the form of the many corporate fraud cases to have surfaced during the late 1980s and the early 1990s: Polly Peck; Barlow Clowes; Guinness; Ferranti; the Bank of Credit and Commerce International (BCCI); Robert Maxwell and the Mirror Group Newspaper pension fund; and others. And such cases should not, of course, be seen in isolation from each other: on 27 December 1992 the *Independent on Sunday* published a full-page chart in which all of those companies were linked together and, in turn, linked to the arms-to-Iraq Supergun affair and the US Iran–Contra deal in an amazing clandestine network of international trade and politics. And several British government departments were clearly implicated in that particular network.

However, regulatory bodies such as the Bank of England and the Department of Trade and Industry had minimal success in preventing the development of this network of deception and incompetence. And in each of these cases the press and broadcast media sat on the sidelines and merely generated endless retrospective analyses of events after they had occurred. Little, if any, investigative journalism took place to expose the seemingly endless stream of fraud and corruption cases of the time. This was not entirely surprising given that much of the British media – particularly the popular tabloid newspapers – was, and still is, content to be overwhelmed by trivial consumer tat and the endless outpourings of the growing public relations industry. The British Establishment must have been very grateful for that: knighthoods and seats in the House of Lords, for example, are seldom awarded to editors of independent and critical newspapers.

In case we need reminding of the very real human cost of official secrecy in this country, we should consider the many major accidents and disasters that took place in the UK during the same period, including those involving the *Marchioness* pleasure cruiser on the River Thames; the Clapham Junction rail crash; the King's Cross underground fire; the capsize of the *Herald of Free Enterprise* ferry at Zeebrugge; the Bradford football stadium fire; and the Manchester aircraft fire. In each of those cases the official bodies responsible for public safety – including the Health and Safety Executive and the Marine Accident Investigation Bureau – were aware of the hazards before the tragedies took place. But in each case all evidence of the risks was kept secret from the public. Thus, some 350 deaths could have been prevented if the public – and therefore the press – had been entitled to inspect official documents relating to public safety and accident prevention.

However, during this period of growth in corporate fraud, political corruption and official secrecy there had been a vigorous campaign for constitutional reform in the United Kingdom as this unacceptable state of affairs had not escaped the attention of opposition political parties, civil liberty pressure groups, think tanks, the voluntary sector and the quality end of the press and broadcast media. The problem, it seemed, is that the United Kingdom has no written constitution or other consititutional provisions – such as a Bill of Rights and a Freedom of Information Act – to challenge this institutionalized secrecy and contribute to the advancement of democratic values. Various campaigns were launched during that period – including the establishment of the pressure group Charter 88 – to press for constitutional reform, and the campaign was a partial success in that it gained positive manisfesto commitments from the main opposition political parties.

The only problem was that such manisfesto commitments failed to become government policy as the respective political parties failed to win successive general elections. And although there is absolutely no political axe to be ground here (investigative researchers and journalists have a duty to remain politically detatched and maintain a critical view of power wherever it lies) in the later part of 1994 and early 1995 there were some particularly sinister developments that could indicate the type of resistance which progressive reforms might encounter. In October 1994, the *Observer* newspaper published a major news item entitled 'Blair in forged letter smear' by its political editor Anthony Bevins. The story reported that a forged letter purportedly from the leader of the shop workers' union, USDAW, had been sent to a senior Labour figure in an attempt to smear and destabilize the Labour Party leader, Tony Blair. A month later *The Spectator* magazine published a story about the Literary Editor of the *Guardian*, Richard Gott, linking him to the KGB. The allegation led to Mr Gott's resignation from the newspaper. And in February 1995 the *Sunday Times* – the former flagship of British investigative journalism – published scurrilous allegations suggesting that the former leader of the Labour Party, Michael Foot, had been a KGB contact. The allegation was widely condemned, and Mr Foot immediately protested his innocence and subsequently won a High Court libel action.

However, this may be a taste of the black propaganda and subterfuge to come in the run-up to a general election that could return a Labour government. After all, any government that proposes constitutional reform on the scale contained in the Labour Party manifesto poses a severe threat to many of the institutions and individuals in this country who possess considerable unaccountable power and wealth.

Indeed, a brief review of some of the widely documented problems that confronted the Labour governments of the mid-1970s under Harold Wilson indicates the reception that such progressive reforms can expect. That Labour government – which was largely made up of social democrats and soft-left socialists – was subjected to every dirty trick in the book: forged Swiss bank accounts; allegations of a KGB cell in Downing Street; suggestions of illegal land deals involving cabinet ministers; innuendo about the relationship between Wilson and his secretary (and even talk of a love-child); whispering campaigns induced by mysterious men in pubs around the country; and daily headlines – largely tabloid – screaming about every minor governmental misdemeanour and error. The range of government sleaze and scandal of the eighties and early nineties already detailed here failed abysmally to attract any comparable media treatment.

The events of the pre-1979 period were compounded by the plethora of private armies set up to challenge, if necessary, the perceived excesses of a Labour government – GB 75, the Unison Committee for Action, and Civil Assistance – which received widespread support from the mid-brow tabloids. And we should not forget the long alleged involvement in attempts to destabilize the Wilson government by what has now become the Department Without A Cause – MI5.

It takes little imagination to conclude that we may now be witnessing a renaissance of institutionalized anti-Labour subterfuge which will no doubt become more evident during the period between now and the next election – and thereafter, of course, if Labour wins.

Even if there is a change of government and a Freedom of Information Act is introduced, it is likely that there will be numerous obstacles to the implementation of such reform. For example, the British Establishment's 'Old Guard' – such as the Whitehall mandarins and the other custodians of Britain's medieval institutions – will resist its implementation. Then there is the mammoth logistical problem of opening up every government office of every government department in the land. Thus, the cost of implementing a Freedom of Information Act will be huge in terms both of expense and of jeopardy to the old system and its exponents. And any incoming Chancellor of the Exchequer will be most anxious not to create any major new areas of public spending where such expenditure can be avoided.

An indication of the potential cost of constitutional reform – if such evidence is needed – came at the beginning of 1994 when the Economic and Social Research Council (ESRC) invited applications from academic institutions and research bodies to undertake a research programme 'The ESRC Whitehall Programme: The Changing Nature of Central Government in Britain'. The research programme will take place over a five-year period and cost an estimated 1.9 m. It is realistic, therefore, to estimate that any proposed constitutional reform would be severely delayed by political, strategic and administrative difficulties that, to date, have not been addressed by the politicos advocating those changes.

The good news on constitutional reform, however, is that at the time of writing an independent inquiry into the implementation of constitutional reform has been set up to examine in detail the practicalities and pitfalls of the Labour Party's proposed reforms. Those proposed reforms include:

- A Bill of Rights
- Freedom of Information legislation
- Parliaments for Scotland and Wales
- Regional assemblies for the rest of the UK
- Electoral reform
- Reform of the House of Commons
- A reformed House of Lords
- A statutory code for civil servants
- A Ministry of Justice and reform of the judiciary
- Independent local government

Quite an ambitious programme, and one that clearly has the potential to attract significant opposition from within the British Establishment. The inquiry – which has a budget of £550,000 provided by a variety of philanthropic trusts and charities – states: 'Little thought has been given to ranking [these proposed reforms] in terms of the order in which they might sensibly be brought forward in a legislative programme; and very little to the complexities and interconnectedness of some of these measures. They are viewed by their supporters as a shopping list which can be given to the civil service to sort out.'

In fact the inquiry's governing document opens with the following warning: 'At the next general election constitutional reform is likely to be a central issue. The Labour Party is committed to introducing what Tony Blair describes as "the most extensive package of constitutional change ever proposed": parliaments for Scotland and Wales, regional government in England, a Bill of Rights, freedom of information, reform of the House of Lords and of the procedures of the House of Commons. No serious advance planning has been done on most of these topics; and, for entirely proper reasons, Whitehall is not allowed to think about them until after the election is called'.

The document continues: 'There is an urgent need to assess the practicalities of these different proposals, to explore the connections between them, and to devise a realistic and coherent legislative programme. This will be carried out by an independent and non-partisan inquiry. Its purpose is to ensure that constitutional reform measures have a fair chance of being planned and implemented in a sensible way, unlike previous attempts at constitutional change (House of Lords reform in the 1960s; devolution in the 1970s) which both ended in a shambles. Without advance planning this looks likely to happen again.'

In the meantime, however, the British people have been treated to a series of *Citizen's Charters* and an addition to the honours system called the *Chartermark*. At least the government of the day acknowledged public concern about official secrecy and the lack of open government, but such responses were little more than further glitzy public relations ventures of the kind that so often overshadow political debate. However, the government simultaneously cultivated a really massive expansion of quangos – quasi-autonomous non-governmental organizations. These are undemocratic government bodies that are often packed with political appointees to spend vast quantities of public money (estimated to be between one quarter and one third of all public expenditure) without any public scrutiny or accountability. The system of accountability which is alleged to apply to quangos (and to every other manifestation of secretive government) is the ministerial accountability to parliament – the very same system that took such a battering from the Scott inquiry into the arms-to-Iraq débâcle and other scandals.

The investigative journalist, though, should not be too concerned about party political matters but should endeavour to maintain a sense of independence and detachment, and view all political issues from a pragmatic viewpoint – more about that later. For now, though, the aspiring investigative journalist can rest assured that there will be no shortage of material to investigate, as little is going to change the inherent secrecy that is such a feature of British society. A change of government will not mean overnight

changes to the constitution; it may be many years before the individual journalist or researcher will see any change to the UK's
institutionalized official and unofficial secrecy.

At this stage it is worth defining our subject in precise terms.
What, exactly, distinguishes investigative journalism from other
forms of journalism? Chambers Dictionary defines investigative
journalism as: 'journalism involving the investigation and exposure
of corruption, crime, inefficiency, etc.' The report *Information,
Freedom and Censorship*, published by the international anti-
censorship pressure group Article 19, provides a more detailed
description of the subject: 'Investigative journalism has emerged as a
separate and specialized mode of journalistic inquiry. It involves the
investigation and exposure of corruption, misconduct and mismanagement of government, bureaucracy, the military, etc. with the
purpose of checking this behaviour through informing public opinion. It came to the fore during the Watergate scandal in the United
States but has long been a feature of German journalism as exempli-
fied by *Der Spiegel*. Investigative journalism extends the limits of
public debate and political participation. The emergence of investigative journalism in other countries such as the USSR and Spain
may be viewed as a sign of increasing demands for more openness in
government. Such investigations are often seen as hostile activity. In
other countries, investigative journalism is an alien concept.'

A more functional interpretation of the subject is given in the
authoritative American tome *The Reporter's Handbook – An Investigator's Guide to Documents and Techniques*. Here, the authors
John Ullmann and Steve Honeyman – who are leading figures in
Investigative Reporters and Editors Incorporated – write: 'It is the
reporting, through one's own work product and initiative, matters
of importance which some persons or organizations wish to keep
secret. The three basic elements are that the investigation be the
work of the reporter, not a report of an investigation made by
someone else; that the subject of the story involves something of
reasonable importance to the reader or viewer; and that others are
attempting to hide the matters from the public.'

It is also worth pointing out one significant sub-division
within that definition: the difference between consumer-related
investigative journalism, which focuses upon individual disputes

and conflicts (often resulting in the trite foot-in-the-door television investigations), and conflicts between the individual and the State. The former is often preferred by editors as they have a more immediate dramatic effect and present less risk in political and legal terms; the latter, however, can bring the newspaper or media organization itself into conflict with authority.

The Ullmann and Honeyman three-point definition of investigative journalism will be used throughout this book. In addition to defining the component parts of our subject, it is also important for us to have some idea of what investigative journalism is not.

Investigative journalism is little if anything to do with body microphones, hidden cameras, paid informants or other cloak-and-dagger activities. Sure, hidden microphones and cameras were essential ingredients in *World In Action*'s memorable programme in 1987 exposing the truth behind the private blacklisting agency the Economic League, but the need to use such tactics is certainly rare and exceptional.

Hence, any perceived glamour of investigative reporting is far more in the eye of the beholder than in that of the practitioner. In the words of one member of Investigative Reporters and Editors Incorporated: 'On average it is nine-tenths drudgery, endless hours sifting through mostly meaningless documents, protracted negotiations with defensive bureaucrats, frequent meetings with dry sources and mentally disturbed crusaders, long nights, cold coffee, busted trails, bottomless pits and, occasionally, heady success.'

As Carl Bernstein of Watergate fame stated in a speech to the 1992 InterNation Conference on Investigative Reporting in Moscow: 'Woodward and I have been the subject of a great deal of mythology over Watergate. What we did was the most basic kind of empirical, methodical police reporting.'

And investigative journalism has also little to do with the endless tabloid coverage of the personal lives of showbiz and entertainment figures. After all, if one accepts the Ullmann and Honeyman definition of investigative journalism, then the British Royal family is rarely subjected to investigative scrutiny; they are merely another topic of the popular consumer journalism more frequently associated with pop stars, film stars, soap stars and sports stars. In fact it has been revealed that prominent members of the

Royal family have themselves used the popular tabloid newspapers for their own public relations purposes. On the subject of personal privacy it should be noted that few investigative researchers, using the techniques detailed in this book, would find themselves in conflict with prospective legislation that may reach the statute book in Britain to protect the privacy of the individual. It should primarily be the institutions and organizations that wield power in our society that are the subject of the investigative enquiry – and individuals operating in an *official* capacity. An individual's private life is not *per se* a matter of any public importance. Proposed legal reforms on personal privacy, currently under consideration by Whitehall, will have only a peripheral effect on authentic investigative research and journalism, as the examples cited in the first chapter of this book will certainly demonstrate.

And what is the real state of investigative journalism in the UK following this catalogue of secrecy, sleaze and cover-up?

Following his departure from the *Observer* newspaper in 1991, investigative journalist David Leigh wrote in the *UK Press Gazette*: 'The state of British journalism is the worst that I can remember. When I came into journalism Harold Evans, the *Sunday Times* and the Insight Team were what we all admired. That's all been gone for more than a decade. There's no serious journalism in the *Sunday Times* anymore. It's all consumer tat.'

More recently, journalist Stephen Glover, writing on the demise of investigative journalism, observed in the London *Evening Standard*: 'Because there is so little proper investigative reporting, it is a safe bet that many abuses of power lie unexamined ... the inescapable fact is that investigative journalism is almost always a little alarming to anyone in power.'

Even the president of the influential Guild of British Newspaper Editors, commenting in the preface to its 1988 pamphlet *Officially Secret*, stated: 'The role of the nation's newspapers as public watchdog is being severely blunted by a pervasive, almost institutionalised secrecy in our society.' And the demise of investigative journalism has also been widely debated in recent years. The death of Thames Television's *This Week* programme in 1992 was widely lamented – and it should not be forgotten that it was the *This Week* programme that produced the now-infamous 'Death on the

Rock' programme about the SAS shooting of three Irish Republicans in Gibraltar on 8 March 1988. The loss of Thames Television's ITV franchise is widely held to have been as a direct result of this controversial edition of *This Week* and, if so, is an indication of the lengths to which the British Establishment will go if the investigative journalist oversteps the mark.

Additions to the investigative journalism casualty list in broadcasting include Yorkshire Television's highly acclaimed *First Tuesday* programme, BBC Television's popular *That's Life* series (a mixed blessing, perhaps) and the further marginalization of Granada Television's award-winning *World In Action* programme. The investigative content of the remaining British current affairs programmes with any commitment to the subject is becoming increasingly sparse on the ground as more pedestrian – and thus cost-effective and politically safe – social policy and political issues are covered instead.

A specific model of the decline of investigative journalism in the field of print journalism can readily be constructed. Take, for example, the announcement in May 1993 that the London Borough of Lambeth had engaged in illegal spending on council contracts of some £20 m over a ten-year period – including the cost of violating the council's Compulsory Competitive Tendering requirements. The same local authority over the same period had been subjected to considerable long-term media scrutiny because of a series of controversial policies and equally controversial council leaders – including 'Red' Ted Knight, Joan Twelves and Linda Bellos. The media organizations that turned those into household names clearly overlooked the massive financial irregularities that were taking place right under their noses.

What makes such an oversight unforgivable is that local government is one of the few areas of British officialdom to be bound by freedom of information legislation in the form of the Local Government (Access to Information) Act 1985.

The London Borough of Lambeth, however, is by no means alone in the local government corruption stakes; the 1985 Act has the capacity to expose many cases of local government fraud and corruption – if only journalists were trained in the use of such obscure legal provisions. How, though, might we know that there is such widespread corruption in local government in the UK? Simple: just take a look at the charts published in *The Independent* on 26 and 27 January 1992 showing that 19 of London's 32 local authorities (of all political colours) were at the time under investigation for fraud – or multiple fraud in many cases. Sufficient evidence, it seems, for every newsroom in the country to arm itself with a copy of the Local Government (Access to Information) Act 1985 and the determination to see local government corruption exposed and justice prevail. Surely John Poulson cannot have been the only one to see the rich pickings to be had from local government.

Even the British Establishment has acknowledged that investigative journalism could be employed to expose many of the system's more questionable activities. At the now infamous Matrix Churchill arms-to-Iraq trial at which a mass of government documents was unexpectedly thrust into the public domain on the order of the trial judge, one salient internal MOD memorandum sent to Ministers in 1989 stated: ' ... much of this information can be declassified since all it needs is for an investigative journalist to pull together the threads.' Unfortunately no such investigative journalist did pull together those sensitive threads. This book aims to change all that.

The demise of investigative journalism in this country can be halted only if the spirit of investigative journalism is given the kiss of life as a matter of urgency, and a culture of investigative journalism is encouraged to flourish. Consequently, this book is part of a campaign – already being debated in such publications as the *UK Press Gazette* and the *British Journalism Review* – to do precisely that and to propose the formation of a Centre for Investigative Journalism.

It is anticipated that this proposed Centre would undertake a four-point programme of action: to provide training courses for a range of participants – not necessarily only journalists; to publish a journal and regular briefings on investigative journalism and related topics; to undertake detailed and ongoing research into the subject and its intended targets; and provide a range of consultancy and agency services to ensure that prospective and practising investigative journalists and other researchers have access to appropriate resources and the opportunity to develop their skills.

The training courses should range from broadly accessible one-off training seminars, to post-graduate diplomas and research degrees. However, a programme of education and training along these lines should not only be available to what is perceived as the professional journalist. As has already been suggested, there are many others in our society with a legitimate right to undertake investigative research and to disseminate the results. And the demand for professional training in this field should be vast, given that there are now some 60 academic institutions in the UK offering courses on media and communications-related subjects. That number is currently growing, and the development of franchised course units makes the prospect of training investigative journalists very real indeed.

The publication of a periodical and *ad hoc* briefings on investigative matters should be integral to such a centre. Given that few journalists have yet mastered the complexities of the Local Government (Access to Information) Act 1985, they are unlikely to have grasped the range of statutes, statutory instruments and other provisions that allow the penetration of a range of official and commercial organizations. Briefings on these and other specific areas of investigative research are desperately needed – after all, remember Francis Bacon's maxim: 'For knowledge itself is power.'

A research programme should be established to provide a quantitative and qualitative analysis of investigative journalism in both the press and broadcast fields to assess its continued demise or, perhaps, its renaissance.

And finally, such a Centre for Investigative Journalism should be a key resource centre, providing expertise and resources to a range of users to ensure the development and expansion of a culture of investigative journalism in this country.

The establishment of such a centre in the United Kingdom will be well in line with the pluralistic traditions of the media in our vigorously pluralistic society. We should not lose sight of the fact that we live in a participatory democracy, and that many major social and legal reforms – including votes for women, the abolition of slavery and the decriminalization of homosexuality – have taken place as the direct result of extra-parliamentary pressure. The media have played a key part in many such campaigns, epitomized in 1961 by the formation of Amnesty International. This particular campaign came into being because an English lawyer, Peter Benenson, discovered that a large number of political prisoners were languishing in jails around the world. The *Observer* newspaper agreed to publish a polemic by Mr Benenson entitled 'The Forgotten Prisoners', which appeared on the front page of its review section on Sunday 28 May 1961. Amnesty International was born, and more than thirty years on it is a multinational and multimillion pound organization that continues to campaign for the many thousands of political prisoners around the world who have still to gain their rights and freedom.

And no doubt the likes of the Birmingham Six, the Guildford Four and the many thousands of callers to Esther Rantzen's Childline should also be grateful for the British media's pluralistic tradition and activity in the righting of wrongs. As the Article 19 report proclaimed: 'Investigative journalism extends the limits of public debate and political participation.'

We know that official secrecy continues unabated in this country, and we have a clear idea of the very real cost of that secrecy in human and social terms. At the same time our media institutions are some of the most powerful organizations in our society. It is difficult, therefore, to argue against the proposition that the press and broadcast media have a duty to investigate and publish the truth; to expose abuses of power by those who have power; to safeguard individual civil liberties; and, if necessary, to challenge the status quo. That imposes a huge responsibility on media organizations and those who work in them to act as the unofficial watchdogs of the public interest. That being the case, one gets the feeling that in the run-up to the twenty-first century the public is being let down very badly.

And, just in case anyone needs reminding of the level of official secrecy that still exists in the United Kingdom, here is a list supplied by the government's Cabinet Office – which, ironically, has responsibility for open government – of the statutes that impose criminal sanctions for the disclosure of information:

Abortion Act 1967, Sections (2) 1(c) and (3)
Agricultural Statistics Act 1979, Sections 2 and 3

Agricultural and Horticultural Act 1964, Section 13
Airports Act 1986, Section 74
Anatomy Act 1984, Section 10(6)
Animals (Scientific Procedures) Act 1986, Section 24
Atomic Energy Act 1946, Section 13
Banking Act 1987, Sections 82–87
Biological Standards Act 1975, Section 5
Census Act 1920, Sections 8(1)(a) and (2)
Cerials Marketing Act 1965, Section 17
Civil Aviation Act 1982, Section 23
Civil Defence Act 1948, Section 4(4)
Clean Air Act 1956, Section 26
Coal Act 1938, Section 1(3)
Coal Industry Nationalisation Act 1946, Section 46
Coast Protection Act 1949, Section 25
Companies Act 1985, Section 449
Company Securities (Insider Dealing) Act 1985, Section 2
Competitions Act 1980, Section 19
Consumer Credit Act 1974, Sections 160(4) and 174(5)
Consumer Protection Act 1987, Section 38
Control of Pollution Act 1974, Section 94
Data Protection Act 1984, Sections 15, 19, 20 and Schedule 1,
        paragraph 3
Deep Sea Mining (Temporary Provisions) Act 1981, Section 13
Diseases of Fish Act 1983, Section 9
Electricity Act 1989, Section 57
Employment Agencies Act 1973, Section 9(4)
Employment and Training Act 1973, Section 4(5)
Energy Act 1976, Schedule 2, paragraph 7
Energy Conservation Act 1981, Section 20(8)
Estate Agents Act 1979, Section 10
European Communities Act 1972, Sections 11(2) and 12
Factories Act 1961, Section 154
Fair Trading Act 1973, Sections 30(3) and 133
Film Levy Finance Act 1981, Section 8
Finance Act 1969, Section 58(6)
Finance Act 1989, Section 182(8)
Financial Services Act 1986, Part VIII

Fire Precautions Act 1971, Section 21
Fisheries Act 1981, Section 12
Food Act 1984, Sections 5(3) and 87(5)
Gas Act 1965, Schedule 6, paragraph 9
Gas Act 1986, Section 42
Harbour Act 1964, Section 46
Health and Safety at Work etc. Act 1974, Sections 27(4) and 28
Highways Act 1980, Section 292(4)
Industrial Training Act 1982, Section 6(2)
Industrial Companies Act 1982, Section 47a
Iron and Steel Act 1982, Section 33
Legal Aid Act 1988, Section 38
Local Government Finance Act 1982, Section 30
Local Government Planning and Land Act 1980, Section 167 and
    Schedule 20, part III
Medicines Act 1968, Section 118(2)
Merchant Shipping Act 1988, Section 52(3)
Merchant Shipping (Liner Conferences) Act 1982, Section 10(2)
National Health Service Act 1977, paragraphs 5–7 of Schedule 11
Offices, Shops and Railway Premises Act 1963, Section 59
Police and Criminal Evidence Act 1984, Section 98
Population (Statistics) Act 1938, Section 4(2)
Prices Act 1974, Schedule X, paragraph 12
Public Health Act 1961, Section 68
Public Health (Control of Diseases) Act 1984, Section 62(3)
Race Relations Act 1976, Section 52
Radioactive Substances Act 1948, Section 7
Radioactive Substances Act 1960, Section 13(3)
Rehabilitation of Offenders Act 1974, Section 9
Rent (Agriculture) Act 1976, Section 30(4)
Restrictive Trade Practices Act 1976, Section 41
Rivers (Prevention of Pollution) Act 1961, Section 12
Road Traffic Regulations Act 1984, Section 43
Sea Fish Industry Act 1970, Section 14(2)
Sex Discrimination Act 1975, Section 61
Social Security Act 1989, Section 19 and Schedule 2
Statistics of Trade Act 1947, Section 9
Telecommunications Act 1984, Section 101

Town and Country Planning Act 1971, Section 281(3)
Trade Descriptions Act 1968, Section 28
Transport Act 1968, Section 87
Value Added Tax Act 1983, Section 44
Water Act 1989, Section 174
Weights and Measures Act 1985, Section 64 and 79(7)
Wireless Telegraphy Act 1949, Sections 5, (6)(ii) and 15(4)(c)
Food Safety Act 1990, Section 33(7)
Human Fertilisation and Embryology Act, Section 37(5)

And just how absurd might some of these statutory provisions actually be in preventing public access to official information? Well, here is Section 64 of the above mentioned Weights and Measures Act 1985: 'Information disclosing the identity of the packer of a package or the identity of the person who arranged with the packer of a package to be made up shall be treated as a trade secret.' So now you know.

Chapter one

A Crash Course in Investigative Research

ONE of the key myths surrounding investigative research and journalism is that it is prohibitively expensive or otherwise very demanding in time and resources. In some circumstances this can be true: for example, if the subject of an investigation is based overseas or is otherwise of an international nature – such as pursuing a fugitive like Lord Lucan or a dubious international banking organization – then, of course, that investigation will be very costly in terms of travel alone. Or, perhaps, an investigation that involves extensive scientific research into a particular form of environmental pollution may involve expensive professional fees for consultants or laboratories. But in such a case it is quite possible that one of the environmental pressure groups – such as Greenpeace or Friends of the Earth – or the appropriate local government authority has already done that research.

But in the majority of cases the subject of the investigative research project will be an organization or institution that routinely comes into contact with the public at large – such as law-enforcement agencies, local government authorities, central government departments and the like. And these organizations tend already to be well documented. The process of investigative research, therefore, is a matter of understanding how these organizations and institutions work; the nature of the individuals behind the decision-making processes; the whereabouts of that existing documentation; and the basic methodology for undertaking an investigation. This chapter, therefore, aims to expose the myth that investigative research and journalism is any more costly than any other type of research or journalism. The 'investigative' element is simply an attitude of mind – of not being prepared to be fobbed off by bureaucrats, and being determined to explore in some detail the workings of organizations that wield power in what is, essentially, a democratic society.

The allegation that investigative work is overwhelmingly expensive is often a red herring thrown up by media institutions that are disinclined to undertake investigative work for other, mainly political, reasons. After all, why blow the whistle on your friends and allies?

Here are ten case studies of real investigative research projects, and each gives a rough estimate of the costs (excluding salary or other costs of the researcher's time).

1   The Kent Police Computer

Back in the early 1980s the North Kent Group of the National Council for Civil Liberties (NCCL, but now called Liberty) took an interest in a brief item that appeared in the annual report of the Chief Constable of Kent which announced the intention of the Police Authority to buy a mainframe police intelligence computer for a cool £1.5 million. Up until that point there had been no public debate about the merit, or otherwise, of such an intelligence computer; and apparently there had been no debate or discussion within the Police Authority (a committee of the county council) about the security and 'Big Brother' aspects of such a system. This purchase, incidentally, was being made before the introduction of either the Data Protection Act 1984, or the Local Government (Access to Information) Act 1985 – both of which would have required the police to place important documentation in the public domain.

The North Kent NCCL group wrote to the Chief Constable of Kent setting out its concerns about this type of computerized intelligence system. It also asked a number of detailed questions, such as: what make and model of computer were they planning to buy; what safeguards and checks would be implemented by the constabulary to prevent unauthorised access to the data; whether informal and unsubstantiated intelligence about suspects would be held on the computer; how many files would be held; what scope for expansion was included in the computer system; whether back-file conversion – a process whereby old records would be put on to the computer – was being planned; and so on.

The Chief Constable replied as follows: 'Dear Sirs, I have received your letter of 24th November about my Annual Report for 1979, and note the matters which interest you. I am now writing to let you know that it is not my practice to enlarge upon the Report. Yours faithfully, B. N Pain, CBE, QPM.'

And that, as they say, was that. However, a few weeks after the Chief Constable's letter had been received by the NCCL group, a job advert appeared in the local press – the Kent Constabulary was advertising for a Computer Services Manager to help run their network of computers, including the proposed mainframe intelligence computer. Potential applicants were invited to write to constabulary headquarters for a job description and an application form, and the NCCL group duly responded to that invitation – in the name of one of its activists.

By return of post the NCCL group received a five-page job description which provided them with more information than they would have even expected the Chief Constable to disclose – including an organizational chart of the staff structure; budgets; details of computer memory size; proposed links with central government computer systems; and similar detailed technical information.

Inevitably the NCCL group used this little coup to maximum campaigning effect by issuing a press release and sending copies of the document to the region's press and broadcast media. This generated considerable media coverage in both the local and national press, and subsequent public interest. Questions were even raised on the floor of the County Hall council chamber. But as a result of this publicity the group then received a leaked copy of a hefty 200-page 'Kent Police Joint Computer Project – Detailed Operational Requirement' document from an annonymous mole. This, in turn, generated even further publicity and also the public debate that the NCCL group had originally demanded. But the cost to the local NCCL group was the postage for two or three letters to constabulary headquarters, and the cost of photocopying and mailing a press release – a total cost of no more than a few pounds.

2 The Data Protection Act 1984 and 'quangocrats'

As we will see later on, the Data Protection Act 1984 is a unique Freedom of Information law that provides considerable insight into the workings of large organizations such as government departments and other bureaucracies. This example of the use of the Data Protection Act in the investigative field relates to the debate in the UK at the end of 1994 about the appointment of individuals to 'quangos' – quasi-autonomous non-governmental organizations – which, at the time, controlled the spending of at least one-third of all central government expenditure. Members of quangos are appointed at the discretion of government ministers and without any public consultation or democratic accountability. It has even been extremely difficult for journalists and opposition MPs to discover the identity of the members of some quangos.

The key document in this case is a written parliamentary question and answer, published in the daily *Hansard* report, between the Labour Member of Parliament for Walton, Peter Kilfoyle, and the then Minister for Open Government (the Chancellor of the Duchy of Lancaster, to be precise) Mr William Waldegrave. Mr Kilfoyle tabled a written parliamentary question asking Mr Waldegrave if he ' ... will publish an annual directory of all those appointed to public bodies as listed in the Cabinet Office publication "Public Bodies 1993", to include the names, addresses, remuneration, period of office and political and pecuniary interests of all those so appointed.'

In his answer, Mr Waldegrave stated: 'No. Information on the 42,606 public appointments listed in "Public Bodies" is not held centrally and could only be provided at disproportionate cost.' But this was not quite true. An eagle-eyed journalist – this author, actually – was aware that a section of the Cabinet Office called the

Public Appointments Unit is responsible for the processing of membership applications to quangos. After the publication of the minister's parliamentary answer, the journalist telephoned the Office of the Data Protection Registrar in Cheshire and ordered copies of the Cabinet Office entry on the Data Protection Register (this is a public register, and there's no fee for copies of entries). The entry duly arrived in the post some three days later, and one section of the document – purpose 24 on entry number F0220056 – indeed related to the Public Appointments Unit.

The entry stated that the Public Appointments Unit maintained 'lists of potential candidates for public appointment' and, despite the reply given by William Waldegrave, listed the categories of information held as follows: 'personal identifiers; personal details; current marriage or partnership; leisure activities or interests; membership of voluntary and charitable bodies; public offices held; qualifications and skills; membership of professional bodies; professional expertise; membership of committees; publications; current employment; recruitment details; termination details; career history; trade union and staff association membership; training record; business activities of the data subject; disabilities and infirmities; racial and ethnic origin; political party membership; support for pressure groups; religious beliefs; other beliefs; references to manual files or records.'

So, the cost of collating all this information on quangocrats would not necessarily have been 'disproportionate' as much of that data was already held on the cabinet's computer. A further investigation of entries on the Data Protection Register for other government departments revealed that most Whitehall departments keep their own computerized records of quangocrats attached to their departments. Thus, the pushing of a few buttons by a few bureaucrats could well have supplied much of the information requested by Peter Kilfoyle MP. A subsequent article on this subject by this author appeared in the *Guardian*'s 'Documentary' column on 30 July 1994. Naturally, this information was then supplied to the Committee on Standards in Public Life headed by Lord Nolan.

The cost of this investigation: a photocopy of one page of *Hansard;* and one five-minute telephone call from London to the

Data Protection Registrar's office in Wilmslow, Cheshire – or the price of a stamp for a postal enquiry.

3 Councillors' interests

The activities of local government authorities and their members – otherwise known as councillors – have long been a source of political controversy. This is largely due to the enthusiasm of the popular press which perceives local government as being a microcosm of the political process and of political power. Hence, if you want to investigative sleaze about a political party, home in on the activities of councils run by that party. That is how the term 'Loony Left' came about during the 1980s and 1990s – the popular press took a keen interest in the activities of such councils as the Greater London Council, Derbyshire County Council, Liverpool City Council and the London Borough of Lambeth. Conservative councils such as Westminster and Wandsworth also came under keen public scrutiny, as did the Liberal Democrat controlled London Borough of Tower Hamlets.

Given that local government in the United Kingdom controls a collective budget of many billions of pounds each year, that level of scrutiny is justified. So, then, is the scrutiny of individual councillors. Unlike Members of Parliament, local councillors have a legal duty under the Local Authorities (Members' Interests) Regulations 1992 (Statutory Instrument 1992/618) to register a wide range of personal and business details with the authority of which they are a member – and the law requires that register to be open for public inspection at the main council offices 'at all reasonable hours'. Needless to say, this register should be of interest to a wide range of community activists and journalists who have dealings with their local government authorities.

The details that councillors are required to provide to the council, and which appear on the register, are:

1 A description of any employment, office, trade, profession or vocation carried on by the councillor for profit or gain.

2 The name of the person who employs him or, as the case may be, appointed him to the office, or the name of any firm in which he is a partner.

3 The name of any person (other than the local authority) who has, not earlier than one year before the date the councillor gives the relevant notice under these Regulations, made a payment to the councillor in respect of –
(a) any expenses incurred by the councillor in carrying out his duties as a councillor; or
(b) his election as a councillor.

4 A description of any contract of which the councillor is aware (including its duration, but excluding its consideration) –
(a) which is made between the councillor (or a firm in which he is a partner, or a body corporate of which he is a director or in the securities of which he has a beneficial interest) and the authority of which he is a member;
(b) under which goods or services are to be provided or works are to be executed; and
(c) which has not been fully discharged.

5 The address or other description of any land (sufficient to identify the land) in which the councillor has a beneficial interest and which is in the area of the authority of which he is a member.

6 The address or other description of land (sufficient to identify the land) which the councillor has –
(a) in England and Wales, a licence (alone or jointly with others), or
(b) in Scotland, by informal arrangements, permission, to occupy for a month or longer and which is in the area of the authority of which he is a member.

7 The address or other description of land (sufficient to identify the land) held under a tenancy where (to the councillor's knowledge) –
(a) the landlord is the authority of which the councillor is a member; and
(b) the tenant is a body corporate of which the councillor is a director or in the securities of which he has a beneficial interest or is a firm in which he is a partner.

8 The name of any body corporate where –
(a) that body (to the councillor's knowledge) has a place of business or land in the area of the authority of which he is a member; and
(b) the councillor has a beneficial interest in the securities of that body where –
(i) the total nominal value of the securities in which he has a beneficial interest exceeds £25,000 or one hundredth of the total issued share capital of that body; or,
(ii) if the share capital of that body is of more than one class, the total nominal value of the shares of any one class in which he has a beneficial interest exceeds one hundredth of the total issued share capital of that class.

Although that Regulation is quite complex and technical, it is worth studying in some detail because the actual information obtainable from the register about individual councillors will be much more 'user-friendly', and might even throw some light on the true nature and motives of local politicians. And this can also be a very powerful tool indeed in the campaign against local government corruption.

Attached to the end of the Regulations is a note which states: 'These Regulations require each elected member of a county, district or London borough council, the Council of the Isles of Scilly or the Common Council of the City of London (in England and Wales) or of a regional, islands or district council (in Scotland) to give the proper officer of the council a notice about his (*sic*) direct and indirect pecuniary interests. ... '

However, the regulations have been amended to apply to the new unitary councils that have been set up in parts of England and Wales and throughout Scotland.

Finally, the regulations note: 'By virtue of section 19(2) of the Local Government and Housing Act 1989, a member of a local authority who fails without reasonable excuse to comply with the requirements of these Regulations, or who knowingly or recklessly provides false or misleading information in a notice under these Regulations, is guilty of an offence.'

But how do the regulations work in practice? A few days before the Lord Mayor's Show in the City of London in 1994, a journalist working for the *Guardian* called into the offices of the Corporation of London – the local government authority for the City of London since 1215 – to inspect the register of members' interests there. It was quite an eye-opening experience too.

The Corporation's members are made up of 25 Aldermen and 123 Common Councilmen who form its main assembly, the Court of Common Council: officially, none of the members is party political. The journalist picked a number of entries from the register at random which revealed a series of curious details. The entry for one Andrew Patrick Withy MacLellan, the council member for the Walbrook Ward, describes Mr MacLellan as a 'retired army officer' with shareholdings in Smiths Industries, Shell Transport and Trading, Inchape, Marks & Spencer and Great Universal Stores. The only other information registered for this councillor was under the 'nature of interest in land' heading. The details given were stated as 'Joint share, as a tenant, of a room' at 228 Bishopsgate, EC2.

This seemed like remarkably modest accommodation for a retired army officer serving on the Corporation of London's Court of Common Council, and so our intrepid *Guardian* hack investigated the given address. It turned out to be a run-down Victorian building opposite Liverpool Street Station, and the ground floor premises housed a picture-framing shop. A side entrance which led to the upper floors was locked and appeared not to be in use. The proprietor of the ground-floor shop confirmed that the address was used by a number of councillors as an accommodation address. Curious stuff.

So the journalist checked Mr MacLellan's address in his *Who's Who* entry which, in addition to stating that this retired army officer had served a stint as Keeper of the Jewel House at the Tower of London, simply gave his address as c/o Bank of Scotland, London Chief Office, 38 Threadneedle Street, London, EC2P 2EH.

What about the *Municipal Year Book* – the definitive directory of local authorities and their members? This gave Mr MacLellan's address as Byways, Lyne Lane, Lyne, near Chertsey, Surrey, KT16 0AN. This is obviously his home address. *The Guardian* also checked his name in the *Masonic Year Book*. This revealed that Mr MacLellan is in fact Major-General A. Patrick MacLellan CB, MBE, a former Grand Steward of the Masonic fraternity. But this entry gave no address.

The journalist then checked out the details of another council member selected at random – one Dr Peter Bernard Hardwick. His register entry showed that he is a consultant anaesthetist at the Royal Free Hospital in Hampstead, north London; and is also a 'Private Medical Practitioner, 6 Devonshire Place, London, W1N 1HH' and a 'Consultant Anaesthetist (Self Employed)'. Neither of these addresses is in the City of London. The register of members' interests reveals, though, that Dr Hardwick's entry of 'land in the area of the authority' is as a leaseholder of basement storerooms at 4 London Wall Buildings, London, EC4, and that he is a 'lessee of the Corporation of London'.

The man from *The Guardian* then visited the office block located at 4 London Wall Buildings in order to contact Dr Hardwick. The concierge there said that they did not know a Dr Hardwick but did sometimes receive mail for someone of that name which they always returned to the Post Office marked 'Not known at this address.'

An article about this case duly appeared in the *Guardian* on the morning of the Lord Mayor's Show, pointing out, incidentally, that neither Major-General MacLellan nor Dr Hardwick was acting in any way illegally or otherwise wrongly in their actions. An individual is entitled to become a councillor for a local authority even if their only link with that area is the rental of a basement storeroom or the joint tenancy of a room in a run-down building. Equally, though, the press is entitled to report in detail the nature of a councillor's interest in the area he represents – just as the public has a right to know. This investigation also usefully details how an individual's identity can be verified from a number of different published sources.

The cost of this investigation: the inspection of the Register of Members' Interests is free; photocopies of the relevant entries from the register were provided without fee (although the council could have made a 'reasonable' charge for them); and the only actual cost was the bus fare to the Corporation of London's main offices in the City of London.

4   Public at risk from defective vehicles

During 1994 and 1995 the headlines reported a number of major accidents and incidents involving coaches, minibuses and a range of heavy goods vehicles (HGVs) that had been operated on British roads by British companies. It is estimated by the government's Transport Research Laboratory that between 700 and 800 people are killed each year by accidents involving HGVs alone – many of which have mechanical defects. However, evidence obtained during the preparation of this book reveals that the authorities are allowing tens of thousands of death-trap vehicles to remain on the road without any attempt being made to prevent further such disasters from claiming even more lives.

The unlikely origin of this piece of research is a book entitled *Tracing Missing Persons* by Colin D. Rogers and published in 1986 by Manchester University Press. On page 138 of the book appears a table detailing the number of enquiries received by the Driver and Vehicle Licensing Centre (now the Driver and Vehicle Licensing Agency) for the disclosure to third parties of the identities of registered vehicle keepers. The table, which covered the year 1983, reads as follows:

- Central Ticket Office   2,818,000
- Local authorities   1,166,000
- Vehicle manufacturers (safety recalls)   550,000
- Police   393,000

- Insurance companies   45,000
- Other government departments   30,000
- Registered keepers and owners   30,000
- General public   25,000
- Solicitors   8,000
- Non-governmental 'enforcement agencies', e.g. the RSPCA 3,000

The table was originally published in the book as an indication of the uses to which the DVLC could be put in the tracing of missing persons. The outstanding statistic in this table, though, is for 'Vehicle manufacturers (safety recalls)' with a staggering 550,000 applications. The implication here is that there were more than half a million motor vehicles that left the production line in 1983 suffering from safety defects and which were therefore potential death-traps. This could have been a freak year for some reason, or the statistics could have been distorted in some way. Before jumping to any conclusions, it would be necessary to look at a series of historical figures for vehicle safety recalls to see if any pattern emerged. For example, what would be the position on recalls all these years later?

A quick 'phone call to the press office at the Driver and Vehicle Licensing Agency in Swansea revealed that the way in which these figures are compiled had changed in recent years – the responsibility had passed to the government's Vehicle Inspectorate, an executive government agency based in Bristol. A call to Bristol soon established that the agency does indeed compile these statistics and that it also publishes the figures each year. And yes, of course, they would be only too pleased to put photocopies of recent recall statistics in the mail.

The results were alarming. For the year 1992–93 there were a total of 755,242 safety recalls involving all types of vehicle. This included: cars, 728,630; HGV and LGV, 18,220; PSV (buses and coaches), 2,351; and motorcycles, 6,041. But of greater concern than the aggregate total is the 'average per cent response rate from vehicle owners'. What usually happens is that if a vehicle manufacturer discovers a safety defect on a particular model of vehicle, it sends a letter to the owner via the Driver and Vehicle Licensing

Agency. But there is nothing in law requiring the owner or registered keeper to respond to the letter. The Vehicle Inspectorate's table, for example, shows that of the 18,220 H Goods Vs and LGVs subject to recall notices in 1992–93, only 73.5 per cent actually responded. That means that the owners or registered keepers of some 4,828 defective HGVs and LGVs had completely ignored the recall letters from the vehicle manufacturers. And that's a lot of dodgy lorries driving on our roads.

The picture the following year was no better. A total of 666,537 recall notices were issued, including some 253,807 on HGVs. The response rate that year for HGVs was 73.68 per cent, which means that some 66,802 defective lorries carried on trucking regardless.

In other words, these published statistics show a number of factors: (i) that there are hundreds of thousands of defective vehicles leaving the production lines each year that subsequently have to be recalled; (ii) that a sizeable proportion of these vehicles are not returned for inspection or repair, and (iii) tens of thousands of potential death-traps are being driven on our roads right now and with the implied consent of the authorities, which take no action against these vehicle owners or operators.

This discovery is a scandal of mammoth proportions; but what is particularly disturbing is that the hazards highlighted here have not been reported in the press or media – although the information is so readily available. Indeed, this material would make a classic investigative piece that would be worthy of the front page of a quality Sunday newspaper committed to investigative journalism. Clearly, there are few of those about these days. And the cost of this piece of research? Two 'phone calls: one from London to Swansea; one from London to Bristol – no more than a pound or two.

5 Scandal buried in National Audit Office reports

No self-respecting journalist or researcher would spend time reading an annual report by a government organization with a name like the National Audit Office. And the government knows it –

which is why one *should* read such reports by the likes of the National Audit Office, however dull it may sound. It would appear that the British government is highly skilled in the manipulation of the media: clearly, it believes that if it wants to prevent the press and public from obtaining highly damaging governmental information, then that information should be published in the middle of an extremely dull document relating to an extremely dull-sounding department. And the ploy usually works. The National Audit Office is an example of just how that manipulation can be used to good effect by official bodies.

In fact, the National Audit Office has published some of the most revealing and, at the same time, damning information about the activities of central government in recent years.

The National Audit Office describes itself as a department of 'investigative accountants' and states that its key work is ' ... the examination of matters of waste, extravagance, weakness in control and general "value for money" '. As we shall see in the section on central government, some high-profile scandals have been exposed in the reports published by the National Audit Office.

But there have also been several major investigations of substantial irregularities that have not made it on to the news pages or the news bulletins simply because the information is buried deep inside official reports that no-one has bothered to read.

Take, for example, the formidable annual report of the National Audit Office for 1992. On page 8 appears a short paragraph headed: 'Property Services Appropriation Account 1990–91'. That sounds dull enough. But the one paragraph of text printed under this heading is a real eye-opener. It reads: 'There was uncertainty whether charges totalling £65.6 million for works expenditure had been properly incurred, and the extent to which the Agency's clients had accepted these charges. There were also difficulties in recovering costs from United States forces based in the UK; weakness in financial control over security furniture; and inaccuracies in charges for directly employed labour'.

That paragraph must be the ultimate understatement. But the section there that surely jumps from the page is the reference to the US forces: 'There were also difficulties in recovering costs from United States forces based in the UK ... ' Could this be the same

USA with which the UK had such a long-standing special relationship? The same USA headed by Ronald Reagan who was so close to
our own Premier Margaret Thatcher? It would seem so. But there is
no mention in that one sentence of how much was owed to the UK
government by our American cousins; or why it had not been paid;
or to what the payments relate. So, how do we find that out?

The first step is to make a 'phone call to the press office at the
National Audit Office. They are helpful, do a little scurrying around,
and then return with the news that the responsibilities of the now-
defunct Property Services Agency have been taken over by the
Department of the Environment. The next port of call, it seems, is a
major reference library with a thorough stock of government reports
and publications – Westminster Reference Library in this case.

Endless documents published by the Department of the Environment have to be ploughed through. Eventually, at the bottom of
page 67 of the *Department of the Environment Published Accounts
1991–92* (published by Her Majesty's Stationery Office, 22 October
1992, £9.35) appears this passage: 'The PSA's responsibility for
United States forces based in this country were taken over by the
MOD [Ministry of Defence] in 1992. They have inherited an outstanding debt of £1.457 million, although it was as high as £12
million at one stage. The debt is now part of a bi-lateral agreement
between the two governments.'

This is quite astonishing: our special relationship with the
USA obviously was not special enough to encourage the USA to pay
its bills on time for basing much of its Cold War nuclear capability
on British soil. And the passage implies that negotiations to settle the
matter broke down at an administrative level and required a bi-
lateral governmental agreement to be established before the matter
was resolved.

Given the political tensions surrounding the issue of American bases in this country during the later part of the Cold War, this
information would have been political dynamite had it been reported at the time. Both journalists and anti-nuclear campaigners would
have been in a position to use this information as a lead for further
research into the nature of this major dispute between the two
countries – such research could then have been advanced by asking

a sympathetic Member of Parliament to table parliamentary questions about the matter. That would have provided additional material, not available elsewhere, for an article or campaign.

Another remarkable passage from the National Audit Office annual report for 1992 reads: 'Legal Aid Administration Appropriation Account 1990–91.' Another particularly dull heading – but wait for this: 'There was uncertainty as to the propriety and regularity of £333 million spent on legal aid. We have not been able to establish that the statutory provisions relating to the award of criminal legal aid, and the determination of contribution orders, were being properly applied by magistrates courts.'

Again, this is another astonishing revelation that never made the newspapers, but should have done so. It is surely unacceptable that the law courts responsible for dealing with some 95 per cent of all criminal cases, the magistrates courts, were unable to comply with the law relating to legal aid – to the extent that £333 m of legal aid simply was not assessed and collected from defendants.

The message of this example of investigative research is that the evidence needed for your research might be lying around in a public library just waiting to be found. Do not be fooled by the appearance of boring, staid official documents that no-one in their right mind would want to read.

The cost of this exercise: one 'phone call to the National Audit Office; the bus fare to Westminster Reference Library; and two sheets of photocopying – no more than £2.

6   BR's dirty little secret on the line

Here's a tricky question: when is an official secret not an official secret? Answer: when it's a British Rail report on the health hazards associated with the flushing of train lavatories directly on to the railway tracks, which has been kept locked in a British Railways Board filing cabinet for the past forty years or so.

One such report, *The British Transport Commission Report on Track Pollution Problems*, was commissioned in 1956 following a complaint from a German flower-seller standing on the platform of a Sussex railway station. He experienced the full thrust of a lavatory being flushed as a Blue Pullman – predecessor of InterCity trains – travelled through the station at high speed. The familiar notice 'Do not flush lavatory while train is standing at a station' gives a hint as to the mechanics of train lavatories.

The flower-seller raised the matter with his Member of Parliament who, in turn, raised the matter on the floor of the House of Commons. Parliament duly instructed the British Railways Board to conduct an investigation into the health implications of this unsavoury practice – a practice still followed on 80 per cent of British Rail rolling stock to this day. The sixty-page report was never made public but, the public was assured, there were no health hazards associated with the dumping of raw sewage in this way.

However, the report – which was obtained by this author using tactics to be outlined a little later – is a damning indictment of this practice, and identifies the health hazards as: 'food poisoning; typhoid and paratyphoid fevers; bacillary dysentery; anterior polio-myelitis; infective hepatitis; gas gangrene; tetanus; and helminthic infections (worms)'.

At the time of the parliamentary intervention, British Rail seemed to take the matter very seriously indeed: the engineering division of its research department at Derby spent three days flushing vast quantities of whitewash down a train lavatory, while technicians carrying sheets of black card ran alongside the train in order to assess the velocity of the liquid distributed in this way.

In fact, the report reveals that BR took the investigation of sewage disposal so much to heart that it even obtained information about the practice in other countries – Belgium, France, Germany, Sweden, Switzerland and the USA. Unfortunately, it did not know what to do with the information once collated: 'Since the journeys on Belgian trains are of short duration, the extent of the problem is considerably reduced.'

But the report demonstrated that it is not only BR staff working on the tracks or passengers standing on platforms who are at risk. 'Organisms were detected in the air in the immediate vicinity of the train and in the air of the vestibule of a coach of a train. It is almost certain that contaminated air can enter the carriages if the windows are open. There is almost certainly contamination of the water supply of kitchens and buffet cars, which may be a source of danger to the well-being of passengers.'

The report provides detailed information on the extent of the threat to public health: 'The hazard is identified as being ten times the strength of ordinary domestic sewage in municipal sewer systems.' It continued: ' ... 200 grams of faeces were applied to a surface area of slightly less than one square foot; coliform bacteria were recovered from the ballast in appreciable numbers for about seven months thereafter.'

The conclusion in 1957 was that flushing raw sewage on to railway tracks ' ... was out of step with modern ideas of health and welfare' and that 'consideration must be given to the increased use of under-floor equipment in rolling-stock and the handling of contaminated gear by maintenance staff.'

But, in the best tradition of BT altruism and forward planning, the report declared that the solution of the problem was 'that the appearance of the track should be improved largely on the lines of *what the eye does not see, the heart does not grieve for*' (emphasis added). No wonder the secrecy.

How, though, does one get one's hands on a secret report of this nature? First, the existence of the report had not been denied by British Rail, and the fact that it existed but that British Rail had refused to release it for public scrutiny had long gone down in civil rights folklore as an example of just how absurd is the British obsession for secrecy.

Then, this author wrote to the Chairman of the British Railways Board asking for a copy of the report. Dozens of letters passed to and fro in which BR denied that it had any obligation to provide copies of the report to the public: 'This was an internal Research Department report and followed normal practice in that it was not published.'

The writer then researched the law and, in particular, looked at Section 144 of the Transport Act 1968 which requires the archives of British Railways to be made available for public inspection. The Chairman of the British Railways Board insisted that the document was an 'active' file, and not an archive file, and was therefore exempt under the 1968 Act. This writer thought differently, and threatened a private prosecution in the magistrates court if the document was not released. Four days later a copy of the 1957 report appeared on the door mat. Victory – and the matter was widely reported in the national press and in parliament on account of the damning evidence contained in the document. A very real example of why official secrecy should be challenged whatever reasons or excuses are put forward by the bureaucrats.

The cost of this research was based entirely on the postage for a lengthy correspondence with the British Railways Board: somewhere in the region of three pounds.

7 The hidden secrets of the asbestos industry

As we saw in the section on the National Audit Office, it is possible to obtain highly revealing information from published government documents that are already in the public domain – although the information that is of interest to us may not yet effectively be public. This section deals with the bringing together of information from more than one source and combining that information to undertake an investigation of a major social problem. In this case we look at the killer mineral asbestos.

Back in the 1960s it was discovered that exposure to asbestos fibres was the cause of at least two fatal diseases: asbestosis and mesothelioma – both of which are cancers that affect the lungs or their lining. Since this discovery, a mass of legislation and statutory regulations have been introduced by parliament to severely limit and control the use of asbestos in this country. Or so we were all led to believe.

The government agency responsible for enforcing this legislation is the Health and Safety Executive (HSE). If we were to play devil's advocate and assume that all is not well in the asbestos industry – and investigative researchers and journalists should always assume the worst and take a cynical view of such matters – then we might find some evidence of that hypothesis in much the same way as we conducted our investigation into the National Audit Office. The beginning of an investigation into the asbestos industry should therefore start with the scrutiny of the Health and Safety Executive's recent annual reports for information on asbestos (not quite as dull as the National Audit Office annual reports, but certainly longer).

And, like the National Audit Office annual report, the Health and Safety Executive's equivalent for 1992–93 contained a buried clause which suggested that all is not well. On page 63 of this document is a paragraph headed 'Mineral Fibres' which includes the following statement: 'A major new initiative was launched in July 1992 to reduce exposure to asbestos dust during the removal of asbestos insulation. A letter was sent out to every contractor licensed to do this work informing them of concerns over the *lack of progress in the industry towards the use of dust suppression and dust control measures*' (emphasis added).

In an appendix of statistics at the back of the report, the further worrying statement appears: 'Asbestos-related disease – the number of new cases of mesothelioma and asbestosis continue to rise. The growth in the number of new cases of mesothelioma continues; of particular concern is the increase among younger age groups ... There is also some evidence of cases of asbestosis arising from exposure *after* the introduction of the 1969 Regulations.'

Statements of this nature should set the alarm bells ringing – particularly when they are so brief and buried so deep in a lengthy official document. It is one thing to have progressive health and safety legislation regulating a killer such as asbestos; it is another to make it work. Clearly, from these two passages in the Health and Safety Executive's annual report, the legislation is not working satisfactorily. (And one could also question whether the sending out of a letter by the HSE to asbestos-removal contractors actually constitutes 'a major new initiative'.)

Shortly before this research was undertaken, the government had introduced the *Citizen's Charter*, and its allied *Code of Practice on Access to Government Information*. Although these two measures have rightly been criticized by sections of the quality press and the 'freedom of information' lobby for being wholly inadequate, they are not entirely without merit. After all, a measure that gives you something when previously you had nothing, can be acceptable – up to a point.

These disturbing leads in the Health and Safety Executive's report, made it necessary to establish whether the HSE had a policy on public access to its documentation *before* alerting them to this interest in the asbestos issue. This was done by simply writing to the

Director General of the Health and Safety Executive, John D. Rimington, asking for a copy of their policy statement on access to information.

After a few follow-up letters, a document entitled *Health and Safety Commission: Policy Statement on Access to Health and Safety Information By Members of The Public* duly arrived. It was a seven-page document accompanied by a press release dated 5 April 1994 headed 'New Statement Issued on Access to Health and Safety Information'. The gist of its policy is one of 'transparency' (i.e. openness) except in several clearly defined areas: 'where the release of information would prejudice the enforcement of the law or harm safety; where it would harm the proper and efficient conduct of the operations of the Commission or HSE; personal information; commercial confidences; information given in confidence; or where the disclosure would be in breach of a statutory restriction.'

So, off went another letter to the HSE – this time asking for a copy of the letter sent out to licensed asbestos-removal contractors mentioned in the annual report. And, lo and behold, a copy of that letter was duly received a few days later. Obviously the government's *Code of Practice on Access to Government Information* can be used advantageously in some cases – but only if there is the commitment to make it work by the individual department or agency concerned.

The letter in question made the following admissions: 'HM Inspectors are concerned at the lack of progress in the industry towards the use of dust suppression and dust control measures during asbestos removal work. Recent tests during dry stripping of sprayed asbestos without these measures have confirmed that dust levels can approach, and on occasions exceed, the typical maximum exposure levels recommended by the manufacturers of power-assisted respirators commonly used in the industry.'

It continued: 'Experience shows that many contractors are making little or no attempt to use effective dust suppression or dust control measures during this work. ... ' But it also warned: 'HSE has heard reports of asbestos removal work being carried out by licensed contractors using self-employed operatives who have been required to provide their own respiratory protective equipment. A licensed contractor may only sub-contract asbestos removal work to another licensed contractor or to a self-employed person who individually holds an Asbestos Removal Licence. ... '

This would appear to be another piece of investigative research that would be worthy of coverage in a national quality newspaper – particular bearing in mind a report by the National Institute for Occupational Health and Safety (NIOHS) quoted in the *New Statesman & Society* magazine of 10 February 1995. This report challenged the perceived wisdom that there is a minimum 'safe' level of exposure to asbestos. The evidence for this was the death of a Portsmouth woman, Irene Jenkinson, in 1993. She had never worked with asbestos but her husband was a boiler engineer who routinely stripped asbestos insulation. Although he did not bring his overalls home to be laundered, asbestos dust may have been in his hair and on his shoes. The Portsmouth coroner issued a verdict of 'death from industrial disease' on Mrs Jenkinson.

A little more research, though, could be done to develop a story on this subject. It would be useful, for example, to obtain some statistics on the importation and use of asbestos in the UK. A 'phone call to a well-stocked reference library – this time the British Library Business Information Service in Holborn, central London – indicates that the *Minerals Yearbook* (published jointly by the British Geological Survey and the National Environment Research Council) would be a good starting point as, of course, asbestos is a mineral.

After skimming this highly specialised reference for only a few minutes, the researcher found, a table of the import and export of asbestos to and from the UK and obtained a photocopy. The table of statistics provided the following information. In 1992, the most recent year for which data were available, the UK imported 7,192 tonnes of crude and fibre asbestos. Curiously, though, we also imported 3,078 tonnes of *waste* asbestos. But the highest figure in the table was for the importation of 'Articles of asbestos cement, etc' at 71,210 tonnes. The table also shows that UK exports of asbestos and asbestos-related items was minuscule by comparison with the imports. Therefore there is still a huge domestic market for asbestos and products containing it. All this research material provides a good investigative lead, and no doubt more traditional journalistic techniques can be used to build a more detailed picture of the uses to which these vast quantities of asbestos are put.

Once again, we have produced a solid and revealing piece of investigative research by using a few official reports, writing one or two letters to the Health and Safety Executive and visiting a well-resourced reference library. And, once again, the total cost does not exceed a few pounds.

8 Defence secrets – in a library near you

If the prospect of ploughing through endless boring and tedious government publications does not grab you, then try familiarising yourself with the stock of your local reference library. It is possible to find the odd official secret or other confidential document lying around on a library shelf, just waiting to be read.

This happened to a CND campaigner in Devon who was browsing through the reference section of Plymouth library. Tucked away on a shelf she found a file with a childlike drawing of a submarine on the front cover. It bore the innocent and unalarming title *Devonport Public Safety Scheme* – or Devpubsaf for short – and had been published by the Royal Navy's flag officer for Plymouth.

Few, if any, of the naval city's 250,000 inhabitants would have known that this document was there for all to read. And yet the hundred- page document revealed what would happen if there were a nuclear accident on a Navy submarine in Devonport dockyard. The Navy had in fact placed 22 copies of the document in the reference sections of public libraries throughout Devon and Cornwall, but without telling anybody.

The front page of one section bore the words: 'This scheme is unclassified but its distribution, in whole or part, should be limited to persons concerned with public safety on a "need to know" basis.' The intricate plan – drawn up by Navy experts in conjunction with local authorities, the police and the other emergency services – went into considerable detail. It revealed that stocks of iodine pills were held by the city's Environmental Health Officer, ready to be rushed to local schools and community centres for general distribution. There were plans to evacuate people from the immediate danger area, and the document stated that schools, hotels and holiday camps would be designated for accommodating these 'refugees'.

The document also spelt out the radiation risk to crops in the countryside around Plymouth, and carried the script of television and radio messages to be broadcast in the event of such a nuclear incident. The first indication of a mishap would be a statement from the Admiral, the flag officer for Plymouth. A message would then be broadcast to the effect that: 'We have been asked to make the following announcement: an incident has occurred in the reactor plant of a nuclear submarine berthed at _____ which has resulted in the release of a small quantity of radioactive products. There is no possibility of a nuclear explosion occurring. Precautions are being taken in certain areas to protect persons against risk to their health arising from the release. The areas affected are ... '

The public would then be asked to take various protective measures which might include leaving the affected area. Advice would include: 'Stay indoors as far as possible; do not eat any exposed food; do not drink any liquids from containers that have been open for more than one hour; tins and containers must be washed thoroughly before they are opened; wash all crockery, cutlery and cooking utensils before use; wash your hands before preparing food and drink, and wash them again before serving it.'

Devonport is one of the few naval bases left since the run-down of Portsmouth, Chatham and others, and is the home port for its nuclear-powered hunter-killer submarines. It also houses the Navy's submarine refitting complex where the core of submarine reactors are removed and replaced. But Devpubsaf insists that a disaster similar to Chernobyl could not happen.

'It is impossible for a reactor accident to result in an atomic bomb type explosion. Current estimates are that we should experience this sort of occurrence no more than once in anything between 10,000 and 1,000,000 years of reactor operation.'

The document reassuringly goes on to say: 'Given that the total number of RN reactor operating years to date is less than 200, it will be appreciated how unlikely are the chances of such an incident. None the less, there must always remain some chance, however small, of an occurrence happening at a time when a nuclear powered submarine is berthed alongside in a port.'

Although submarine hulls are designed to form a 'secondary containment' in the event of an accident, the document explains: 'there must always be the chance of an open hatchway or other external venting allowing the fission products to escape to the outside atmosphere when they will tend to form a cloud which may thereafter be borne along on the prevailing wind.'

The document then tells us that 'if an accident led to a vessel sinking, the fission products would be released into the sea, but would be dispersed by prevailing currents and would not be a significant hazard to health.' The document says that in any accident it would be essential that personnel be evacuated, first from inside the area at risk, approximately 50 metres around the submarine's hull. But if radioactive material were released into the atmosphere 'it is unlikely a health hazard will exist beyond 550 metres from the vessel. However, within this range these particles will represent a separate and distinct hazard to health.' So now you know.

This case indicates just how public some defence secrets can be, and spies can often save themselves the indignity and inconvenience of engaging in espionage by simply using an appropriate reference library. This was the message from the British Library Patent Service following a break-in at the Farnborough Air Show in 1988. The national press reported an investigation by the Ministry of Defence police of the night-time break-in at the airshow in which an American prototype fighter-pilot helmet was dismantled and photographed. It was not known whether the culprit was a conventional spy or someone engaged in industrial espionage.

However, the British Library made the following point in a leaflet promoting its patent services: 'The industrial spy who staged a raid at the Farnborough Air Show to steal the secrets of a new helmet for fighter pilots could have saved himself the trouble – and fulfilled his mision legally. The patent was freely available at the British Library!'

But back to the cost of obtaining the Devonport Public Safety Scheme document: the document was freely available for public inspection, and the cost of photocopying its 100 pages (at an average cost of 10 pence per A4 page) would be a staggering £10 – by far the most costly piece of research examined so far!

9 NHS secrets for sale

Here is a vivid example of just how true is that ancient maxim 'For knowledge itself is power'. Back in 1990, senior officers of the Medway Health Authority announced that they were planning to raise a little cash – £10,000 to be precise – by selling mailing lists of certain patients to mail order companies and other junk-mail brokers.

The lists in question were of the parents of children who had been immunised or vaccinated against disease. The theory was that the parents of such children are particularly responsible parents, and would therefore be of great interest to companies wanting to promote such services as health insurance policies, life assurance and the like. The proposal was raised at a meeting of the district health authority, following which a major and controversial political storm broke out.

The local newspaper ran the front-page healine 'Secrets for sale – fury over deal for kiddies health care list', and the proposal was denounced by the local Community Health Council as 'unethical'. The CHC secretary was quoted as saying: 'If it means that the district [health authority] intends selling the names and addresses then we would be very concerned. It is unethical. I would not want that sort of information about my family sold to a third party without my permission.'

He added: 'It's a basic tenet in the health service that information such as names and addresses and dates of birth are confidential and should not be forwarded to a third party without permission – if that is what the district intends to do, then it's not permissible.' But what the Community Health Council did not know at the time was that the proposal was also illegal under the Data Protection Act.

A few days after the story broke, the newspaper printed a letter from a local civil rights lawyer which explained: 'The Data Protection Act 1984 regulates the use of personal information held on computers, and it is almost certain that the Medway Health Authority holds its lists of children on a number of computer databases. Indeed, all mail order companies only buy mailing lists that are held in this easy-to-use format.'

The letter continued: 'Data Protection Principles 2 and 3, which form part of the 1984 Data Protection Act, state: "Personal data shall only be held for one or more *specified* and lawful purposes" and "personal data held for any purpose or purposes *shall not be used or disclosed in any manner incompatible with that purpose or purposes.*"' The letter then went on to outline the role of the Data Protection Registrar's office in investigating complaints and enforcing the law in cases of abuse by a data user.

The following week the newspaper carried a report entitled '"Secrets for sale" fear quashed', explaining that the local health authority had not really been planning to sell the list of names and addresses at all, but had only been planning to sell the data to general practitioners 'so that they could check against their own records to ensure that all children were immunized'.

Therefore the views and informed comment of a couple of articulate citizens can force a huge, multi-million pound bureaucracy to engage in a policy about-turn simply by presenting well-researched information to the appropriate media. And, as with the earlier section on government quangos, the cost of obtaining information from the Data Protection Registrar is the cost of a 'phone call or a postage stamp.

10 Secrecy in the courts

The final word goes to the North Kent group of the National Council for Civil Liberties whose campaign on the Kent Police Computer we examined at the beginning of this chapter. The group's impressive track record covered a range of campaigning issues in the areas of 'official secrecy' and 'freedom of information', and one of its campaigns in particular even went on to make legal history.

It all started when a short letter was published in the *Guardian* from a Geoffrey Allen of Penge in south-east London. It read: 'Tom Sharratt (*Education Guardian*, November 11) states that "everyone has the right to know who holds office in a local community including magistrates ... " That seemed obvious to me also, until I recently attempted to discover the identities of local magistrates. I was informed that it is official policy at Court House,

Bromley, not to reveal the names of local magistrates. No doubt the same policy is applied in many areas of the country, so it seems that we have a largely secret judiciary – yet another example of the obsessive secrecy in British public life, hardly consistent with democracy. Yours faithfully ... '

This was effectively an invitation for the civil liberties group to swing into action, and it duly proceeded to write to each of the magistrates' courts in its area – about eight in all – asking for a list of the names and addresses of the magistrates serving each division. In each case the Clerk to the Justices replied that this information was not available to the public and they were therefore declining the request for information.

The NCCL group then wrote to the Lord Chancellor at the House of Lords asking two key questions: first, is there any statutory or common law provision requiring or prohibiting the publication of JPs' names and addresses?; and secondly, would the Lord Chancellor state if the public is entitled to know the names and addresses of magistrates serving in Kent?

Sir Bryan Roberts of the Lord Chancellor's Department responded with the following answer: 'There is no statutory provision either prohibiting or requiring the publication of the names of Justices of the Peace. A general list of local justices is normally available at any courthouse, and the only reason why the identity of justices in a particular area might not be revealed to a person or organisation would normally be a risk that the information was required in order to facilitate harassment, intimidation or other threats or dangers to the magistrates concerned. Such a problem sometimes arises in a particular case, where a dissatisfied litigant seeks personal retribution against the bench concerned.'

Sir Bryan continued: 'In short, therefore, any person or body should be entitled to know the identity of the members of the local magistracy, unless there is some manifest reason in the public interest to refuse it in the particular case.'

The NCCL group was then able to obtain a copy of the *Justices' Handbook* – the county's *Who's Who* of local magistrates, detailing the name and address of each – from the county council's Magistrates Courts Committee. This was clearly a major victory in challenging and overturning an established practice of official secrecy. But the significance of the letter from the Lord Chancellor's Department did not end there.

A few years later the *Observer* newspaper became involved in a legal case over the policy of the Clerk to the Justices in Felixstowe in refusing to provide the press with the names of magistrates dealing with a particular case. The journalist involved, and the *Observer* newspaper, then made an application to the High Court for an order of *mandamus* instructing the clerk to name the magistrates. The case naturally attracted considerable media attention as it was seen not only as a case relating to the reporting of court proceedings, but also as a matter of principle about the rights of the press and the public to know the identities of public officials who wield significant power on behalf of the public.

At the High Court hearing, the letter from Sir Bryan Roberts to the North Kent NCCL group was a central piece of evidence submitted by the journalist and the newspaper. The case was won by the applicants, and the court ruled that the identities of magistrates should normally be made available to the press and public. A few years later, in a speech to the Magistrates' Association, the Lord Chancellor referred to this case and stated that Sir Bryan Roberts's letter had been instrumental in the court's decision to allow the press and public access to the identities of magistrates. Therefore, a small campaign, launched by a small group of committed individuals, resulted in a change in the law. Every individual in our society, it seems, has the power to challenge the status quo, and to encourage the implementation of progressive change at all levels.

Conclusion

Every major social reform that has ever taken place in our society has taken place as the result of extra-parliamentary pressure – often from very ordinary individuals who have somehow been motivated to press for change. And most such campaigns have involved the use of the press and broadcast media, as discussed in some detail in the introduction. If the maxim 'For knowledge itself is power' is true, then the process of investigative research is absolutely central to the process of social change – as we have seen in this chapter.

48: *Lifting the Lid*

And in case any aspiring investigative reporter is a little concerned at the lack of glamour associated with the process of investigative research, let us once again ponder the sacred words of America's two leading investigative journalists, John Ullmann and Steve Honeyman: 'On the average, it is nine-tenths drugery, endless hours sifting through mostly meaningless documents, protracted negotiations with the defensive bureaucrats and lawyers, frequent meetings with dry sources and mentally disturbed crusaders, long nights, cold coffee, busted trails, bottomless pits and, occasionally, heady success.'

Happy hunting.

Chapter two

The Tools of the Trade

IN order to successfully undertake an investigative research project it is necessary to be aware of a number of positive traits that should ideally be present in the professional investigative researcher or journalist. And it is also necessary to have an understanding of the range of other skills and resources – both human and mechanical – that will be useful, if not essential, in order to progress the investigative project and assist in the development of the research.

The most successful researchers (and the same can be said of lawyers, accountants, academics and anyone else who handles vast quantities of paper) are often those who are efficient administrators; who set up and operate well-organized filing and information-retrieval systems; and, in case of emergencies, also have reliable memories. After all, a press cutting that contains essential information on your particular subject of inquiry is of little use if it cannot be located; and the world's greatest expert on your particular subject will be of no help to your campaign if you have lost his or her name and telephone number.

Therefore, here we err on the side of caution and assume that everyone is a beginner, and we also advise that the seemingly obsessive procedures outlined in this chapter for the recording and storing of information are observed as closely as possible. The individual researcher will no doubt find his or her own preferred level of efficiency – although this might change on the day that a crucial clipping or document goes temporarily astray.

Personal traits – inherent or acquired

The most important personal trait that must be possessed by anyone undertaking investigative research or journalism – whatever the reason or motive – is personal integrity. Such a trait is usefully combined with objectivity, tenacity, a sense of morality and an overwhelming compassion to pursue all the facts that are necessary for establishing a substantial truth.

Specifically, the motivation behind the researcher's actions should include the following elements:

• A controlled sense of outrage at the corruption, misconduct, conflict of interest or just plain mismanagement in the various organizations and institutions in our society that wield power, and a general understanding of how such organizations function, in order to pinpoint specific injustices or crimes.

• The acknowledgement that the best chance of success in investigative research is through a fair and ethical investigation that lacks any hint of party political interest. The researcher should understand that it pays to be honest and ethical, and acknowledge that any illegality or dishonesty is dangerous to the researcher and the cause or causes in which they have an interest.

• A strong belief and conviction that an honest, direct and balanced approach is the only way to deal with sources and investigative subjects, and is also the only way to ensure credibility as an investigative researcher (and, indeed, as a journalist or campaigner). This should include an understanding that the intended audience of the research – which will often be the public at large – will be offended and disillusioned if a reporter or campaigner misuses the power of the media by engaging in deliberate distortion, or engaging in the sensationalism that is too often present on the news and features pages of many of our newspapers.

• Patience and confidence that an honest, persistent and systematic enquiry will eventually unearth the truth or otherwise provide evidence of maladministration, misconduct, corruption or some other malfunction of an official body or private institution.

• The ability of the researcher to stand back periodically from the object of the enquiry and view it in human terms: has the researcher been fair in his/her dealings with the sources of the research and, indeed, with the object of the research itself?

• The ability and willingness of the researcher to admit that he or she has made a mistake and was wrong on a matter of fact or perspective; and to take the necessary steps to correct the record without delay where there has been a significant error or distortion of the truth.

These are indeed very high standards for the investigative researcher to meet. But given the apparent levels of injustice and corruption that exist, or have existed, in our society (remember thalidomide, the Birmingham Six, the Bank of Credit and Commerce International, the Maxwell pension fund, the sinking of the pleasure cruiser the *Marchioness*, etc, etc, . . .), there is no need to invent or distort the research. In other words, there is injustice and corruption out there – you just need to go out and find it.

Personal knowledge

The investigative researcher will at some stage come into contact with a wide variety of official bodies and bureaucracies, and the investigative journalist will inevitably come into contact with such organizations at all levels on a routine basis. Therefore the following is a general checklist of areas of knowledge and understanding that the researcher will need to develop as time goes by or, if necessary, learn at very short notice.

• A general familiarity with the various forms of local and central government – including district, county, unitary and regional councils; and central government and quangos – and the ability to analyse basic issues associated with conflicts of interest, maladministration and corruption.

• A general familiarity with the law as it deals with the operation of revenue – particularly in local government, the voluntary sector and companies – and the ability to find a way around a balance sheet and other financial documents and accounts.

• A specific understanding of the basic records kept on individual subjects by the State – such as registers of births, deaths, marriages, divorces, land ownership, councillors' interests, company directorships, etc.

• A working knowledge of the few Freedom of Information laws that do exist in this country – particularly the Local Government (Access to Information) Act 1985 – and those laws and regulations that allow the public to inspect background official documents.

• A thorough knowledge of the various types of pressure group and campaigning organization associated with the extracting of official information from state and local bureaucracies, and also of those concerned with the righting of individual or collective injustices. These include Justice, the Campaign for Freedom of Information and Public Concern at Work. And find out about their local contacts or groups, if any, in your locality.

• A general understanding of the courts system applying to both civil and criminal matters – including the obtaining of court documents on debts, bankruptcies, coroners' reports and the like.

• A specific understanding of the role of law-enforcement agencies in addition to the police, such as the local authority Environmental Health Department, the Crown Prosecution Service, the Data Protection Registrar, Serious Fraud Office, Customs and Excise, Department of Trade and Industry Investigations Division and other regulatory bodies.

• A general understanding of the operation of both Houses of Parliament, and also local government authorities, in relation to their legislative and investigatory functions –

particularly their oversight of the jurisdiction of those bodies (including the House of Commons Select Committees such as the Public Accounts Committee).

• General familiarity with the daily *Hansard* reports – including the reporting of parliamentary debates and the publishing of written parliamentary questions and answers – and the way in which local government authorities keep their minutes and background reports.

• A general understanding of electoral law and election procedures, and the legal availability of background details and election accounts of each prospective councillor and each prospective Member of Parliament.

• A working knowledge of the investigations and operations of the National Audit Office (for central government) and the Audit Commission (for local government), and the manner in which their published reports can serve as authoritative background material on maladministration, misconduct and corruption in central and local government authorities and agencies. This knowledge should include an understanding of how National Audit Office and Audit Commission investigations are launched, and how to carry out a thorough investigation of what information may be available from these agencies in any specific case.

• Background knowledge of the history of scandals involving central and local government (e.g. the Poulson case, the Westminster cemeteries scandal or the arms-to-Iraq cover-up) together with an understanding of the role – or lack of it – of the media in advancing the subsequent investigations.

• Background reading of successful and unsuccessful investigations, at both local and national levels, to learn the nuts and bolts of the planning, strategy and analysis of major cases of scandal or other wrongdoing. For example, *All The President's Men* by Carl Bernstein and Bob Woodward (Futura Quartet, 1975) provides a detailed insight of a well-known criminal investigation. Nearer home, *Death of a Rose-Grower – Who Killed Hilda Murrell?* by Graham Smith (Cecil Woolf 1975) examines the noticeable contrast between a police murder investigation, and that subsequently undertaken by a range of journalists in one particularly controversial case.

• An understanding of press ethics and the laws of contempt, in order that the investigative reporter or campaigner does not enagage in any activity that could prejudice an investigation by a law-enforcement body or, worse still, that results in civil or criminal proceedings against such an investigative reporter or campaigner. This should include some understanding of the rules of evidence and admissibility.

This list should not be seen as too alarming, as much of this information is contained in the various chapters of this book. But do not be deterred from reading up on any of these topics from other sources, too.

Methodology

There are few rules about investigative research of more value than the general guideline 'follow the paper trail', and the researcher who does precisely that is the researcher who will come up with the most thorough research and, in the case of journalism, the best investigative articles. The intellectual exercise that the researcher embarks upon well before any research is undertaken is often the key to a successful investigative project. It is a process of calculating where the appropriate documentation might be found, and how to legally access that documentation, that is often pursued rigorously by experts in the investigative field.

American investigative reporters often recite the mantra 'follow the dollar'. In this country we should coin the phrase 'follow the pound'. It is an obvious proposition, but one that is seldom considered by campaigners and journalists: if a public official is involved in corruption, misconduct or a conflict of interests, then there is one likely reason for it – financial gain. Or, conversely, if there is a suspicion of good old-fashioned maladministration in a public body, this will lead to one inevitable conclusion – financial loss. So the key to an investigation may well be financial documentation.

Although many journalists will claim to be better at words than figures, they should take every opportunity to improve their understanding of accounts and other financial documents. For example, under the Local Government Finance Act of 1982 each local government authority is required to have its accounts audited each year by an independent firm of accountants. During this process, the local press and public has the right under Section 17 to 'inspect the accounts to be audited and all books, deeds, contracts, bills, vouchers and receipts relating to them, and make copies of all or any part of the accounts and those other documents.'

This must be the most revealing 'freedom of information' law in the UK and one that is grossly underused; it is a pity that no such provision applies to central government accounts. However, given the scope of local government corruption in the light of the tens of billions of pounds spent each year by local government authorities, then this particular legal provision is likely to be of considerable use to the investigative researcher. And that is a very good reason why it is invaluable to develop a working knowledge of accounts and other financial documents. However, it is important to remember that although such financial records may be a key lead in an investigation, it will be necessary to use other sources of information too, such as council minutes and interviews with, possibly, council officers or the elected representatives themselves.

Plans and chronologies

Researchers who follow the paper trail or otherwise undertake detailed investigative research should adopt a systematic approach to their work and to the organizing of the mountains of paperwork that will inevitably grow as the investigation gets underway and progresses.

And any research project will benefit from the production of a plan or outline before the research starts. This will be particularly useful as a focus for the direction of the project and prevent distractions that may arise as the work progresses: certain types of personality can be easily distracted by the range of facts, figures and documents that this type of investigative work throws up.

An example of a research outline could relate to a local authority suspected of having acted fraudulently over the sale of a plot of land. The outline might look something like this:

1 What initial evidence exists that gives rise to the suspicion that there might be an irregularity over the sale of this plot of land? And how reliable is that source?

2 Housing Committee/Planning Committee minutes: what references are there to this plot of land in the minutes of these committees over, say, the past two years?

3 What background council documents are *now* available under the Local Government (Access to Information) Act 1985 for public inspection that were not available at the time of the sale or other transaction?

4 Are there any entries on the Statutory Planning Register indicating a change of use or change of ownership that helps our research?

5 Should we check back copies of all local (and regional) newspapers for any reference to this property during the past, two years? (These are available at the local reference library.)

6 Do we know a helpful and co-operative councillor on the appropriate council committee who could exercise his or her legal right to obtain more detailed background information?

7 Are there any independent experts on this subject in any local groups or organisations such as Shelter, a squatters' action group or a housing co-operative?

8 The Land Registry: do we need to go to the modest expense and inconvenience of doing a search of the Land Registry to establish ownership, registered mortgages, etc?

This list provides the researcher with a useful outline of the work that will need to be done on this project, and also provides an idea of the location of the various sources of information, which, in this case, will mainly be the local reference library and main council offices. The outline will also be useful for assessing the time that the research will take to complete.

There are two particularly helpful publications that show how to plan a research project. The first is the trusted *Citizen Action – Taking Action in Your Community* which is edited by Des Wilson (Longman, 1986). A section entitled 'Getting The Facts' by Maurice Frankel details how a research project is put together and provides a mock-up of a research paper. A more recent publication, which is primarily aimed at academic researchers (although it is easily applicable to non-academic research) is *The Research Project: How To Write It* by Ralph Berry (Routledge, 3rd Edition 1994) which is a stage-by-stage guide to project work, and covers such topics as taking notes, shaping and composing the project, writing cross-references and a bibliography, cataloguing systems and on-line databases, etc. It is highly recommended.

Filing

The best policy is to keep all papers that you accumulate during the course of your research – even if only for a limited period for eventual weeding out at a later date. You are invited to take the word of an experienced researcher who earnestly believes that there is nothing more frustrating than to recall a piece of research undertaken at an earlier date which has since been thrown out – only to be subsequently considered as having some importance. Clearly a distinction has to be drawn between retaining useful documents and becoming something of a hoarder. That, of course, is a matter of individual judgement which it takes some time to acquire.

However, a system needs to be introduced for the most effective and reliable storage of the documentation that is obtained during the course of research. Given that most documents and photocopies will be of A4 size (210 mm by 297 mm, or 8.27 inches by 11.69 inches), using A4-size ring binders or lever-arch files is the best bet. This allows for access to individual documents whilst retaining the remainder in chronological order. Bulky documents, such as bound volumes of council minutes or background reports, can be stored in banker boxes or even just old cardboard boxes of an appropriate size.

Note taking

If one is to believe that efficient filing is important in the retrieval of documents (and it is), then the same applies to notes. Professionals who undertake complex research – such as solicitors engaged in court proceedings – will keep a detailed note of every meeting, 'phone call and conversation, and have those notes typed up and filed away for future reference. One reason for this is that solicitors get paid by the minute, but it also enables them to be one hundred per cent sure of the facts of the particular case in hand. There is a lot to be said in favour of such a system, however time-consuming it may be, as such detailed notes add considerable authority and credibility to the research.

For example, it would be difficult for a bureaucrat or official to rebut or contradict a conversation if a contemporaneous note has been kept by the researcher, together with a note of the date and time of the conversation or call. Here is an example of a file note, as they are called in legal circles, made by the author, of a telephone conversation with a representative of the Campaign Against the Arms Trade (p.59).

Given the damning nature of the subject, and the revealing information to have come out of that telephone conversation, one can see the benefit of a punctilious approach to note-taking. Another approach, often favoured by professional journalists and broadcasters, is to use a sturdy A4 spiral-bound notebook as a diary file. Simply, a note is kept of every conversation, interview, telephone call or other detail in chronological order, and the same notebook can be used for more than one research project, as the researcher will be clearly able to distinguish between the various entries.

It is advisable to date and time each entry, for example: '29/5 – 12.35 pm: telephoned the Chief Executive on 010–101 to enquire about the availability of the Housing Committee minutes. She was not available, but her secretary said that the C/Ex will return my call either this afternoon or tomorrow morning.' And all of the pages

FILE NOTE

From: DN

To: File

Date: 5th October 1993

RE: ARMS EXPORTS

1 Telephoned the Campaign Against The Arms Trade on 0171–281 0297 and spoke to ANN FELTHAM who is going to send me some bumpf in the post.

2 Re £5.2 b exports from UK: we are now 6th in the international league table of arms exporters – were 4th not long ago. Most of our exports are to Saudi Arabia and Malaysia.

3 There are some 80,000 applications for licences to export arms and arms-related products from the UK each year. The authorities (i.e. Customs and Excise and the Department of Trade) '... don't even pretend to police the exports once they have left the country.'

4 Re. registers of arms: the CAAT is calling for a public Arms Export Register to be set up to monitor in detail such exports. The UN Register has just been set up and is retrospective – runs from April of this year. Very vague and unrevealing – only contains a few catagories of heavy weapons; CAAT and the House of Commons library have copies.

5 Re. the Iraqi arms build-up: the CAAT knew about them in the 1980s 'but nobody was interested'. Even very few MPs were interested until the war and subsequent Matrix Churchill furoré. There is a freelance journalist, Alan George, who has done a lot of in-depth probing into such matters.

6 The CAAT has a substantial press cuttings library that goes back to the 1970s.

should remain intact in the notebook, even when they are history, as you never know when you might need that information again or, indeed, the Chief Executive's direct-line telephone number. Another advantage of this style of note-taking, incidentally, is that it can be an insurance policy against libel or other legal proceedings. If one is able to state with precise certainty the detail of every conversation or other aspect of a research programme – with material evidence in support – then one is certainly able to give a very credible account of events.

Resources

Experts

It is always useful to assume that someone, somewhere has the information that you are seeking; and that lurking somewhere in the land is an expert on that particular subject. Such an assumption could save you a considerable amount of time and inconvenience in duplicated research. There are several ways of tracking down such experts. The first is an amazing directory called the *Directory of British Associations* which lists some 7,000 groups and associations covering every conceivable subject (and many inconceivable subjects) and is an invaluable source of such expert information. It is published by CBD Research Ltd, and stocked by many reference libraries as a key reference work. Another useful source is the 'News Contacts' directory published each week in the *UK Press Gazette* – the journalists' journal. The directory lists hundreds of contacts in companies, utilities, charities, government departments, organizations and the like.

In the field of scientific research, a charity called the CIBA Foundation operates the Media Resource Service on 0171–631 1634 and 0171–580 0100 and describes itself as 'an independent service provided free to science and the community'. It operates a database of more than 5,000 experts who have agreed, in the first instance, to provide background information or unattributable comment to the media on topics in the areas of medicine, technology and science. Experts on a variety of other subject areas are detailed throughout this book.

61: *The Tools of the Trade*

Libraries and specialist libraries

It is advisable to get to know your local library service in as much detail as time allows. The examples of investigative research detailed in Chapter One provide vivid examples of just what type of incriminating material can be found simply lying around on a shelf waiting for someone to pick it up. Bear in mind that even a small branch library will be part of a county-wide or borough-wide library service, and information can be transferred from branch to branch with considerable ease. Try also to become familiar with the library's catalogue (especially if computerized); any databases it operates or to which it subscribes; the local studies collections; information on local clubs and societies (this might well include information on the subject of your research); and their press cuttings files. Although most library services will keep back-copies of local newspapers in their archives, they may also keep separate files of press clippings on individual local dignitaries such as councillors, Members of Parliament, business people and others. Play it by ear, and sound out just how extensive their records and archives are. Librarians usually appreciate enquiries from researchers who have a respectable and organized quality about them; however, they live in dread of library-users who create havoc with their stock. So the tactful cultivation of contacts at your local library could be a very worthwhile investment.

There are also hundreds of specialized libraries and library collections across the country. These are detailed in the definitive publication on the subject, the *Aslib Directory of Information Services of the United Kingdom*, to which all libraries will have access. Another fine source of archive material is *British Archives – A Guide to Archive Resources in the United Kingdom* by Janet Foster and Julia Sheppard (Macmillan Reference Paperbacks, 1984). This is particularly useful, as it lists most county and borough archives – including such material as old birth, death and marriage records – and their various specialist collections.

Photocopying

Few researchers will have the benefit of their own photocopying facilities – although most staff journalists will have this facility in-house. It is useful to keep a note of the opening times of local stores and libraries that offer photocopying facilities so that you know where, exactly, to go if you urgently need to do some photocopying on a Sunday afternoon. Keep an eye open for the growing number of retail outlets (mainly newsagents) that now offer cheap photocopying at 4p per copy. If a journalist or other expert takes an interest in your research project or campaign, make it a golden rule *not* to hand over your original research – even on a temporary basis. Only ever supply photocopies of your work, as it can be stated with some dismay that even successful journalists working for renowned press and broadcasting organisations have the amazing capacity to lose, mislay or accidently mis-file other people's work. You might never see it again.

Faxes

Again, get to know the whereabouts of the various commercial fax machines in your locality. As with photocopying, keep a note of the opening hours and charges so that you can keep costs to a minimum. Remember, even if you do not own a fax machine, everyone else will assume you do. You cannot escape them.

Microfiche and microfilm readers

You will, from time to time, come across data that is available only in microfiche or microfilm format. For example, this particularly applies to Companies House records where all documents are supplied in microfiche format. That's no problem during the time that you are actually at Companies House, as they have banks of fiche readers which can print out hard copies of the documents. But once you get the fiche home it is another matter, as each document on the fiche is about half the size of a postage stamp. Your local library may have a fiche reader; otherwise local educational institutions such as a college, adult education centre or tech. may be able to help.

Computer research system

There appear to be few professional or commercial information systems that are not on-line (that means available on a

computer network). But such systems usually come with an expensive price tag and are, therefore, out of the reach of most researchers.
While such systems can be extremely useful, bear in mind that the
type of material that frequently dominates investigative research
will not be on such a system: council minutes, government reports,
press cuttings, and the like. So, unless you have unlimited financial
resources, it is advisable only to access databanks that are free or to
which a library service subscribes.

Basic reference sources

It should be stressed that basic reference sources can contain
a wealth of information that is easy to overlook, and which could be
extremely useful to an investigative researcher. An example of that is
Whitaker's Almanac which provides seemingly endless lists of state
officials, judicial office-holders, honorary big-wigs and other pillars
of the Establishment. Another example is *Who's Who* which lists
many tens of thousands of individuals, many of whom are particularly specialist or local in their nature. Even the local telephone
directory and electoral register should become a trusted source of
information for the seasoned investigator. Indeed, the research
systems that will count most in your investigative project will be the
research systems or sources immediately available to you. Get to
know them well.

Chapter three

Ethics and Law

THE former Prime Minister, Baroness Thatcher, was once a whistle-blower against official secrecy in the UK. In 1960 she championed a parliamentary bill to open-up local government meetings to the press and public – the bill went on to become the Public Bodies (Admission to Meetings) Act 1960. During the parliamentary debate on the bill in the February of 1960, the young Margaret Thatcher told the House of Commons: 'The paramount function of this distinguished House is to safeguard civil liberties rather than to think that administrative convenience should take first place in law ...'

However, her premiership oversaw a number of major cases of censorship, official secrecy and press restrictions. These included the ban on broadcasting Sinn Fein spokespersons; the *Spycatcher* and Ponting cases; the Cavendish affair; and attempts at prohibiting such programmes as *Death on the Rock, Zircon, My Country Right or Wrong, Real Lives*, and others. At about this time our country witnessed the range of corruption cases, sleaze, misconduct and maladministration that have been mentioned earlier, and which have become the political hallmarks of their time.

So, in the light of these severe difficulties, what ethical considerations should investigative researchers and journalists have in relation to their work of uncovering official and unofficial secrets? Part of the answer is contained in the personal traits outlined in Chapter 2 of this book. But it is also useful to examine various codes of practice and other guidelines that exist in the world of journalism and whistle-blowing for further guidance.

As there are a number of such codes, the investigative researcher is in the unenviable position of having to mix and match a code of practice to suit his or her own needs and considerations. It is appropriate for the investigative researcher to look at ethical standards that apply to the press and broadcast media as most forms of investigative research will be intended for eventual publication. Therefore the codes of practice set by various media organisations would be the appropriate standards for the investigative researcher to use. We start by looking at a simple but effective code of practice adopted by one American newspaper, the *Cincinnati Enquirer*:

- The identities of all sources of information must be verified and confidentially disclosed to the editor.

- Misleading information about the true identity of a source may not be used in a story, even to 'throw off' suspicion.

- Information supplied by an unnamed source should be verified independently or confirmed by at least one other source. An exception may be made for individuals who are the sole possessors of the information or whose integrity is unassailable.

- The motive of the anonymous source should be fully examined to prevent the journalist being unwittingly used to grind someone's axe.

- The journalist should avoid using anonymous sources for information that calls someone's judgement into question or for statements that are a matter of opinion.

- Information attributed to an anonymous source must be factual and important to the story. Peripheral information or 'a good quote' are not good enough reasons for anonymity.

- When an unnamed source must be used, the story should explain why their identity is being withheld, and enough information given to establish their authority to speak on the subject.

- The journalist should not quote people whose identities he or she does not know or cannot verify.

The National Union of Journalists' own Code of Professional Conduct for media workers in the United Kingdom and Ireland also tackles a number of ethical considerations of importance to the investigative researcher. It states:

- A journalist has a duty to maintain the highest professional and ethical standards.

- A journalist shall at all times defend the principle of the freedom of the Press and other media in relation to the collection of information and the expression of comment and criticism. He/she shall strive to eliminate distortion, news suppression and censorship.

- A journalist shall strive to ensure that the information he/she disseminates is fair and accurate, avoid the expression of comment and conjecture as established fact and falsification by distortion, selection and misrepresentation (*sic*).

- A journalist shall rectify promptly any harmful inaccuracies, ensure that corrections and apologies receive due prominence and afford the right of reply to persons criticized when the issue is of sufficient importance.

- A journalist shall obtain information, photographs and illustrations only by straightforward means. The use of other means can be justified only by overriding consideration of the public interest. The journalist is entitled to exercise a personal conscientious objection to the use of such means.

- Subject to justification by overriding considerations of the public interest, a journalist shall do nothing which entails intrusion into private grief and distress.

- A journalist shall protect confidential sources of information.

- A journalist shall not accept bribes nor shall he/she allow other inducements to influence the performance of his/her professional duties.

• A journalist shall not lend himself/herself to the distortion or suppression of the truth because of advertising or other considerations.

• A journalist shall neither originate nor process material which encourages discrimination on grounds of race, colour, creed, gender or sexual orientation.

• A journalist shall not take private advantage of information gained in the course of his/her duties, before the information is public knowledge.

• A journalist shall not by way of statement, voice, or appearance endorse by advertisement any commercial product or service save for the promotion of his/her own work or of the medium by which he/she is employed.

This Code of Professional Conduct not only provides some idea of current ethical standards in journalism, but is also useful for the researcher or campaigner to bear in mind when dealing with representatives of the press and broadcast media, as it is binding on many of those journalists and broadcasters.

By far the best code, however, is the current Press Complaints Commission Code of Practice (which replaced the Press Council Code of Practice): it is thorough and explicit, and should be followed by anyone undertaking investigative research.

The PCC code of practice

1 Accuracy

(i) Newspapers and periodicals should take care not to publish inaccurate, misleading or distorted material.
(ii) Whenever it is recognized that a significant inaccuracy, misleading statement or distorted report has been published, it should be corrected promptly and with due prominence.
(iii) An apology should be published whenever appropriate.
(iv) A newspaper or periodical should always report fairly and accurately the outcome of an action for defamation to which it has been a party.

2 *Opportunity to reply*

A fair opportunity for reply to inaccuracies should be given to individuals or organizations when reasonably called for.

3 *Comment, conjecture and fact*

Newspapers, while free to be partisan, should distinguish clearly between comment, conjecture and fact.

4 *Privacy*

Intrusions and enquiries into an individual's private life without his or her consent are not generally acceptable and publication can only be justified when in the public interest. This would include:

(i) Detecting or exposing crime or serious misdemeanour.

(ii) Detecting or exposing seriously anti-social behaviour.

(iii) Protecting public health and safety.

(iv) Preventing the public from being misled by some statement or action of that individual.

5 *Hospitals*

(i) Journalists or photographers making inquiries at hospitals or similar institutions should identify themselves to a responsible official and obtain permission before entering non-public areas.

(ii) The restrictions on intruding into privacy are particularly relevant to enquiries about individuals in hospital or similar institutions.

6 *Misrepresentation*

(i) Journalists should not generally obtain or seek to obtain information or pictures through misrepresentation or subterfuge.

(ii) Unless in the public interest, documents or photographs should be removed only with the express consent of the owner.

(iii) Subterfuge can be justified in the public interest only when material cannot be obtained by any other means.

In all these clauses the public interest includes:

- Detecting or exposing crime or serious misdemeanour.
- Detecting or exposing anti-social conduct.
- Protecting public health and safety.
- Preventing the public being misled by some statement or action of an individual or an organization.

7   Harassment

(i) Journalists should obtain neither information nor pictures through intimidation or harassment.

(ii) Unless their enquiries are in the public interest, journalists should not photograph individuals on private property without their consent; should not persist in telephoning or questioning individuals after being asked to desist; should not remain on their property after having been asked to leave and should not follow them.

The public interest would include:

- Detecting or exposing crime or serious misdemeanour.
- Detecting or exposing anti-social conduct.
- Protecting public health and safety.
- Preventing the public from being misled by some statement or action of that individual or organisation.

8   Payment for articles

(i) Payments or offers of payments for stories, pictures or information should not be made to witnesses or potential witnesses in current criminal proceedings or to people engaged in crime or to their associates except where the material concerned ought to be published in the public interest and the payment is necessary for this to be done.

(ii) 'Associates' include family, friends, neighbours and colleagues.

(iii) Payments should not be made either directly or indirectly through agents.

9 *Intrusions into grief or shock*

In cases involving personal grief or shock, enquiries should be carried out and approaches made with sympathy and discretion.

10 *Innocent relatives and friends*

The press should generally avoid identifying relatives or friends of persons convicted or accused of crime unless reference to them is necessary for the full, fair and accurate reporting of crime or legal proceedings.

11 *Interviewing or photographing children*

(i) Journalists should not normally interview or photograph children under the age of 16 on subjects involving the personal welfare of the child, in the absence or without the consent of a parent or other adult who is responsible for the children.

(ii) Children should not be approached or photographed while at school without the express permission of the school authorities.

12 *Children in sex cases*

The press should not, even where the law does not prohibit it, identify children under the age of 16 who are involved in cases concerning sexual offences whether as victims or as witnesses or defendants.

13 *Victims of crime*

The press should not identify victims of sexual assault or publish material likely to contribute to such identification unless, by law, they are free to do so.

14 *Discrimination*

(i) The press should avoid prejudicial or pejorative reference to a person's race, colour, religion, sex or sexual orientation or to any physical or mental illness or handicap.

(ii) It should avoid publishing details of a person's race, colour, religion, sex or sexual orientation unless these are directly relevant to the story.

15   Financial journalism

(i) Even where the law does not prohibit it, journalists should not use for their own profit financial information they receive in advance of its general publication, nor should they pass such information to others.
(ii) They should not write about shares or securities in whose performance they know that they or their close families have a significant financial interest, without disclosing the interest to the editor or financial editor.
(iii) They should not buy or sell, either directly or through nominees or agents, shares or securities about which they have written recently or about which they intend to write in the near future.

16   Confidential sources

Journalists have a moral obligation to protect confidential sources of information.

Following the Calcutt recommendations to introduce laws prohibiting the use of bugging devices by journalists and broadcasters, a new clause was introduced in 1993 as follows:

Listening devices

Unless justified by public interest, journalists should not obtain or publish material obtained by using clandestine listening devices or by intercepting private telephone conversations. The public interest defence will operate in this clause as elsewhere in the Code.

A further amendment was made to the privacy clause: private property is defined as any private residence, together with its garden and outbuildings, but excluding any adjacent fields or parklands; in addition, hotel bedrooms (but not other areas of an hotel) and those parts of a hospital or nursing home where the patients are treated or accommodated.

Anyone engaged in investigative research, for whatever purpose, should develop a thorough understanding of the Press Complaints Commission Code of Practice and apply its standards as the absolute minimum ethical standard acceptable to their work.

Code of practice for whistle-blowers

Finally, a further code of practice that will be extremely useful to the investigative researcher is a code for whistle-blowers published in *Minding Your own Business* by Marlene Winfield (Social Audit, 1990). Its code provides the following advice:

Prepare yourself mentally

1. Ask yourself, is the practice clearly illegal or potentially dangerous or is it simply a questionable business policy? Is the public interest really at stake? Be sure you are not acting prematurely. Be sure of your motives and that personality conflicts, career disappointments or self-gratification are not affecting your judgement.

2. Be realistic about the potential human damage caused by blowing the whistle – damage to the company, its shareholders, its clients, your colleagues. Be realistic about what you are likely to achieve. It is quite possible that the organization, even if proved wrong, will suffer less than you do.

3. Be optimistic but also be prepared to lose – the battle, your job, your security – and to be rejected by colleagues and friends and probably see your family suffer. Consult with your family, explain your case, and try to win their support. Be frank in acknowledging that they may suffer.

Prepare your case

1. Identify the issues carefully and prioritize them. Analyse the grievance; identify who will suffer if the problem goes unchanged and how much suffering will occur. Be able to speak knowledgeably about the costs of inaction.

2. Know and be able to refer to the ethical standards of your professional association or trade union if you belong to one. Identify the laws and regulations which relate to the abuse. Identify organizational mandates, official policies, statements of mission and philosophy which support correcting the abuse.

3. Document everything thoroughly and double-check your information. Gather statistics, memoranda or other data to support your position. Make sure you are right.

Exhaust internal channels first

1 Develop an action plan. Take your complaint in writing, using as appropriate supporting documents for everything that you disclose, to the authorities of your company or agency. Ask them to correct the abuse and give them fair warning that you may go outside if this is not done.

2 Exhaust all internal channels, making sure that your efforts to do so are well-documented. This is by far the best method of choice for resolving the problem – if there are channels through which you will be given a fair hearing.

3 Give the organization time to remedy the situation before going further. Try to be flexible and realistically patient; whistle-blowers tend to develop a rigid response.

Protect yourself

1 Try to enlist others in the organization to join you. Concerns carry more weight if they are shared.

2 If possible, approach someone higher up in the organization as a sounding board and to keep you informed of what is happening. Be sure it is someone you can trust and whose advice you respect.

3 Stay on your best behaviour with superiors and peers. Work hard and do your job thoroughly. Bear in mind that all of your past performance may be reviewed if you blow the whistle; and that those you expose may retaliate or try to discredit you.

4 Know your legal rights and contact a good employment lawyer or someone who can advise you on your legal position. You should examine whether or not you are likely to be breaking any laws or terms of contracts by the action you choose.

5 Look for another job. Even if you are right, and even if you are not sacked, you will almost surely lose the trust of your employers.

Go outside only if there is no alternative

1 If all internal channels fail, you have several options: resign and speak out; stay and try to expose the abuse anonymously; stay and go public; stay and say nothing more. In any case, the benefits must be weighed against the likely risks.

2 You may choose to take your complaint to an appropriate statutory agency, or expose it through the media, or go to a pressure group or a Member of Parliament. It is best to go through a person or group who might be able to provide some authority and protection.

3 Focus on the issues and not the personalities involved. Keep to a few key issues. Try to suggest solutions to the problems you have exposed. Know how much you are willing to compromise.

4 Be aware of the difficulties of blowing the whistle anonymously, and if you do, be prepared for your identity to be discovered. Remember that some third parties may not feel able to act on anonymous information, and that it is difficult to pursue a case unless someone is prepared to take up the issue publicly. If possible, go public in a group. Have a plan to keep the issue alive. Do not rely on a single burst of publicity.

5 Keep a log or diary of everything that happens, particularly at work, from the time you decide to take action.

Clearly, much of this advice will be invaluable to the investigative researcher as the subject of the research will invariably be a government department or other official organization. Since this code of practice was published, a law centre for whistle-blowers, Public Concern at Work, has been set up, and can be contacted at: Lincoln's Inn House, 42 Kingsway, London, WC2B 6EN. Telephone 0171-404 6609. Fax 0171-404 6576.

Libel

Libel can be the most devastating legal problem to confront any individual involved in investigative research or writing. Even a letter from one individual to another containing information about a third person can be libelous. The information does not even have to be published in a newspaper or magazine – almost any document, even those supposedly intended only for internal consumption, can contain a libel. And the cost of libelling someone can be excruciatingly high.

In 1983 the House of Lords heard an appeal of a libel action brought by a police constable against an aggrieved suspect (Fraser versus Mirza). The defendant had been arrested by the plaintiff police officer and then released without charge. The defendant then wrote a letter of complaint about the police officer to the Chief Constable of Strathclyde implying that the officer had been motivated by Mr Mirza's racial origin. Only two or three people saw the letter, but the House of Lords decided that it was defamatory, and awarded the plaintiff £5,000 in damages. The defendant would not only have to pay the damages, but also the legal costs for *both* sides – amounting to many tens of thousands of pounds.

The advice, therefore, is to be scrupulously honest and fair with everything that you write down during the course of your research, and assume that it will be published at some stage in the future – even if this is not actually intended. It is worth noting that it is not possible to defame or libel a local government authority, but it is possible to defame or libel a company or other commercial body (such as the notorious 'MacLibel' case brought by the McDonald's fast-food chain in 1994), and a claim for damages citing a loss of profits and/or public goodwill could confront an unsuspecting individual who regrettably says the wrong thing about the wrong individual or organization in the wrong way.

Numerous law books and guides to legal rights cover the subject of defamation and libel, and they invariably advise anyone threatened with legal action to seek the advice of a solicitor without delay. This is very good advice, but lawyers do not come cheap. So it is worth while finding out if there is a civil rights lawyer or law centre in your area that might just be able to provide a little *pro bono* (without fee) advice. And there is considerable merit in the idea of joining a trade union or professional association that provides free legal advice and representation. Otherwise, the definitive works on the subject for the aspiring litigant-in-person are *Defamation* by Duncan and Neil (Butterworth) and *Gatley on Libel and Slander* (Sweet and Maxwell).

Official Secrets Act

Since the demise of the Cold War, and also since the prosecution authorities lost both the Ponting and *Spycatcher* cases, there is little chance of any investigative researcher or campaigner being charged under the Official Secrets Act. If you are charged with spying, or some other aspect of activity covered by the Official Secrets Act, then you will be delighted to know that you will automatically qualify for legal aid. Make sure, however, that you retain a firm of solicitors well-versed in such cases. Advice on this matter is obtainable from the National Council for Civil Liberties on 0171–403 3888.

In short, therefore, adopt and maintain a high ethical standard, and be very cautious about making speculative allegations about any individual or organization. After all, investigative research is all about dealing with facts and the evidence that exists to verify the facts.

Chapter four

Individuals

THERE are two questions that investigative researchers should ask themselves before conducting research on an individual: first, is there a substantial case for undertaking research on that particular individual, or is the research motivated by nothing more than mere curiosity? And the second question should be: is this the *right* individual to be researching, or is there another individual (or others) relevant to this piece of investigative research who should be scrutinized?

For example, a comment made by a councillor in the council chamber in support of a proposed building development might arouse the suspicions of campaigners against the development. But the individual councillor making that statement might only be a policy spokesperson or a mere backbencher trying to impress more senior councillors. Therefore, a considerable amount of time might be wasted in investigating the business interests of that individual and may in fact turn up nothing of any relevance. However, it might be more worth while to look at the membership of the council committee dealing with the planning application – which will probably be the Planning Committee – and find out which councillors are members of that committee. Is that backbench councillor on the Planning Committee? What does the statutory register of councillors' interests show about that councillor and the members of that committee? Is there a press-cuttings file on these councillors at the local reference library? Once these questions have been answered it will be possible to focus in on the research in a systematic and organized way.

In the case of public officials, business people or other individuals engaged in activities of public interest, it is useful to draw up a checklist for each investigation. This might include the following categories of information:

- Date and place of birth.

- Brief family history (particularly if the subject is part of a family active in business or politics) and background of partner/spouse.

- Schools, college or university attended, and details of any academic or professional qualifications.

- Service in any of the armed forces.

- Business directorships and shareholdings. And who are the subject's fellow directors?

- Paid employment and income bracket.

- Voluntary and honorary offices held in charities and organizations.

- Membership of a political party or other political organization and positions held.

- Club and masonic membership.

- Public appointments, such as membership of quangos, health authorities, development agencies and the like.

- Past and present addresses and property ownership details.

- In the case of a business person or professional, who are the main clients?

- Hobbies and pastimes.

- Informal networks and regular meeting places.

- In the case of a councillor, membership of committee and sub-committees.

This checklist would probably only apply to a major investigation, such as that on a politician or prominent businessman, but it is flexible and can be amended to suit the individual investigation.

The next step is to use basic information that is readily available in the public domain.

Who's Who: this huge directory lists the biographies of some 30,000 individuals from all walks of life who exercise power in one form or another – in the arts, business and finance, the Church, the Civil Service, politics, academia, entertainment, sport, the law, local government, the media, medicine, professional institutions, science, technology, the trade unions – in fact, the entire British Establishment is to be found detailed in the 2,131 pages of *Who's Who*. However, many entries are for the not-so-famous who have made an impression at a regional or local level. For example, the leader of a large local authority, or managing director of a regional industrial concern, could well have a modest entry. And this annual directory provides a wealth of information on individuals, such as directorships, hobbies, addresses, family details, education, publications, etc. But the entries are submitted by the individuals themselves, and therefore might be incomplete. It is nevertheless a good and useful starting point.

The International Who's Who: this is the definitive source of biographical information on the world's most eminent and distinguished personalities. It covers the lives and achievements of over 20,000 women and men including heads of state, politicians, religious leaders, ambassadors and diplomats, and prominent figures in the world of business, technology, medicine, law, the arts. Data includes date of birth, nationality, career details, honours, current address and telephone number, place of birth, parentage, marital status, children and leisure interests. There is also a full directory of the world's reigning royal families.

Newspaper records. Always assume that a prominent individual will have attracted some press attention or publicity at some stage in the past. Check with the library service local to the individual's home or business address, or a specialist library such as the City Business Library or a university library. A quick telephone call might establish whether a cuttings file exists on your subject. Another possibility is a call to the librarian at the main office of the appropriate local newspaper, but they are often reluctant to allow public access to their private files. However, by cultivating a journalist contact it might be possible to gain access to a newspaper's records by indicating that a good story could eventually result from the research.

Telephone directories. Check the white pages entry to see what information appears on your subject. If your target has an unusual name then look for alternative spellings. The Yellow Pages and other local directories, such as Thomson's could be a source of information on a business or organization, and your subject's competitors could also provide useful leads. Back copies of all UK telephone directories since 1900 are available for consultation at the British Telecom Museum at 135 Queen Vicoria Street, London, EC4V 4AT. Telephone 0171-248 7444. The local Thompson directory also contains a separate directory of postcodes of large users (including Post Office box holders), and a street-by-street directory of postcodes, which is useful for cross-referencing in a major investigation. And note that the destination addresses for Post Office boxes are not confidential: details are readily available to anyone telephoning the sorting office local to the box's postal code.

Town and city directories. Some areas publish a local directory detailing a wide range of information on all aspects of the town or city in question. The directory publisher Kelly used to publish directories for all major town and cities in the United Kingdom, including details of each street and its inhabitants. But the rising cost of printing, and the routine availability of other information such as telephone directories and the electoral register caused these to decline. However, there are some exceptions. For example, the Kingslea Press Limited each year publishes *The Birmingham Post and Mail Year Book and Who's Who* which is a fascinating cornucopia of local information. The 1994 edition contains facts and figures under the following headings: local government; law courts and magistrates; MPs and election returns; government departments; political associations; trade, industry and professions; law and professional lists; churches, religions, congregations, etc; voluntary and charitable organisations; education and youth; health services; social services departments; cultural activities and entertainments; sports, pastimes and clubs; the forces and ex-service associations; transport and travel; weather; postal information; hotels, restaurants, etc; the City's principal neighbours; Birmingham's neighbours; and Who's Who in Birmingham. Another rare example is the 750-page *Belfast and Northern Ireland Directory* which covers government administration in Northern Ireland; UK government public services; local government; Belfast street directory; Belfast professions and trades; Northern Ireland counties and town directory; and limited liability companies. This is the sort of publication that every town or city would benefit from: regrettably only a handful are published in the UK.

Neighbours. A nosy neighbour can be a great source of information on a subject, and there is no reason why an investigator should not make discreet enquiries if all other avenues fail. Going back to one of the examples of investigative research detailed in Chapter 1, the *Guardian* journalist enquiring about the whereabouts of a City of London councillor found the shopkeeper at an address listed in the register of councillor's interests to be particularly helpful. A discreet and polite enquiry of a neighbour can result in a rebuttal, but quite often the nosy neighbour is on the lookout for a receptive audience.

Electoral register. The electoral register, detailing the names of everyone entitled to vote at a general election, has been published each year since 1830 and is now regulated by the Representation of the People Act 1983. Registration forms are sent out to every residential address by the local electoral registration officer in October of each year, and a draft electoral register is usually available within a few weeks. The final version of the register is then published in February of each year, and is available for public inspection at main council offices or local libraries. Although the electoral register is a useful source of information about the whereabouts of individual residents, it is defective in a number of ways. First, the government's Office of Population Censuses and Surveys have recorded a growing trend in people failing to register or re-register. This trend was encouraged with the advent of the Poll Tax, and it is estimated that up to 2 million UK citizens are absent from the electoral register. The other issue is that an individual is entitled to use an alias on the electoral register, such as an unmarried couple using the same family name for the sake of appearances. However, the electoral register can make fascinating reading. For example, the register for Kensington Palace in London provides detailed information of the living arrangements of some members of the Royal

Family. Apartment 1a is inhabited by Her Royal Highness The Princess Margaret – Countess of Snowdon; Susan E. Andrew; Christine P. Byrne; Sandra Morgan; and Jane Stevens. Apartment 1 is listed as having the following inhabitants: His Royal Highness the Duke of Gloucester; Her Royal Highness the Duchess of Gloucester; the Earl of Ulster; William D. Dorman; Pat J. Fenlon; and Jason R. W. Higginson.

Births, deaths and marriages. Since 1837 the registration of all births, deaths and marriages has been recorded by the General Register Office, and these data are now held at St Catherine's House, 10 Kingsway, London, WC2B 6JP. Telephone 0151–471 4200. It is possible to do a personal search of the indexes to these records at St Catherine House's, which are stored manually and organized in alphabetical order in huge quarterly ledgers. Copies of certificates can be ordered from St Catherine's House once the registration number has been tracked down in the index. It can be a painstaking process, and is usually only necessary in a major investigation of a particularly sinister and evasive individual or network. However, the certificates will contain such information as the name, ages, occupation, address and marital status of the subject. Much of this information is also held locally where the birth, death or marriage was registered. Check in the local telephone directory under 'Registration of Births, Deaths and Marriages' and call the local Superintendent Registrar's office for details of the procedure for undertaking a search of the local registers.

Divorce. A register of all decrees absolute in England and Wales since the 1850s is maintained by the Record Keeper, Divorce Registry, Somerset House, Strand, London, WC2A 2ER. Telephone 0171–936 6000. This is open to inspection by any member of the public. The register contains the full names of the two parties, the date and place of marriage, and the date of the decree absolute. Copies of the decree are also available.

Wills and probate. Since January 1858, copies of all wills and letters of administration have been held at the Principal Registry of the High Court's Family Division at Somerset House. The records are maintained in alphabetical order under the year in which probate is granted, which could be the year of death or the following year. An index of wills and probate is readily available for public inspection, and the corresponding files can be ordered once the reference number is known. The grants of probate and letters of administration generally only contain the name and address of the deceased, details of their personal representative (usually a solicitor or accountant) and the value of the estate.

Court records – civil cases. In County Court actions for debt or damages, it is possible to inspect the Register of County Court Judgements (CCJs), which is maintained by The Registry Trust Limited, 173 Cleaveland Street, London, W1P 5PE. Telephone 0171–380 0133. A postal search can be undertaken for a fee of £5 by supplying the full name and address. If there is a debt registered against that name at that address then the details provided will be the name of the County Court, the plaint (case) number, the date of judgement and the sum involved. The County Courts deal with all actions for debt up to £50,000. Curiously, there is no register of High Court judgements for sums above that figure. The moral of this useful piece of information is that if you are planning to get into debt, then do it in a big way so that no record of the debt shows against your name. In cases of bankruptcy, a register of bankruptcy petitions and receiving orders is available for public inspection at the Thomas Moore Building, Royal Courts of Justice, Strand, London, WC2A 2KJ. Telephone: 0171–936 6000.

Court records – criminal cases. In the United States of America, it is possible for reporters to gain access to a wide range of files in criminal cases. To quote from one handbook on American journalism: 'The case file is obtained from the clerk of the court … in the file you may find an information sheet, complaint, indictment, affidavits, warrants, bail affidavit and receipt, subpoenas, application for warrant, the court docket, and (sometimes) transcripts, lists of exhibits, motions and answers, jury instructions and verdict forms, and final disposition and judgement.' No such facility exists in the United Kingdom. It is entirely discretionary for the police or prosecuting authorities to disclose information about a particular case as they wish to. Indeed, the Queen's Bench Divisional Court of the High Court (in the case of Regina versus Secretary of State for the Home Department *ex parte* Westminster Press Limited) ruled in 1992 that the press has no automatic right to know from the police the name of any person being investigated or who has been charged with a criminal offence. In the judgement, Lord Justice Watkins said: 'The press has no greater right to acquire knowledge of matters of public interest than any other members of the public'. And, of course, the public has no automatic right to that information in the first place. In fact, the law works the other way around: under the Police and Criminal Evidence Act 1984, a police officer investigating a 'serious offence' can obtain an order requiring a journalist to surrender evidence deemed useful to the investigation. This can include written notes, photographs or recordings of taped interviews. It is indeed odd that the press and public are entitled to sit in on most court proceedings in the UK, but have access to no official mechanism that can provide background information to the case or to the defendants.

Coroners inquests. This is another contentious area of the law for the investigative researcher. An unexpected death is required to be referred to the local coroner for an inquest to examine the causes of that death. Such a death is also likely to attract the attention of reporters and others, and it follows that they would find it particularly useful to have access to witness statements and transpcripts of inquests. But that does not always happen. According to the Coroners Act 1988, the coroner has the power – but not the duty – to release copies of such documents to 'properly interested parties', which although not defined in the Act is usually the family of the deceased. The coroner also has the discretionary power to exclude the press and the public from the inquest 'in the interests of national security'. Once again, it is ironic that the press and public can usually attend a coroners inquest and hear the evidence, but have no legal right of access to the documentation. In 1991, *The Independent* newspaper reported a Department of Trade and Industry-funded study into fatal accidents, conducted by the London Hazards Centre, which found that information on nine out of 34 fatal industrial accident inquests in one year was withheld by coroners. The pressure group Inquest, which advises and represents families involved in controversial deaths, has reported that the withholding of information by coroners is common in cases where there is a suspicious death of a subject in police or prison custody. Inquest can be contacted at 330 Seven Sisters Road, Finsbury Park, London, N4 2PG. Telephone 0181–802 7430.

Individuals as companies. Sometimes individuals set themselves up as limited companies to benefit from the tax advantages that relate to companies and company directors. This means that a wealth of information is subsequently available on that subject from Companies House records, which can be purchased for a mere £4.50. A few years ago a political storm broke out over the revelation that the Director-General of the BBC, John Birt, was being paid as a company. This meant that the BBC paid a fee to Mr Birt's company instead of a salary to Mr Birt. This legitimate procedure was disclosed by a journalist who, for no particular reason, was idly tapping famous names into the computerized index of company directors at Companies House in London. The name 'John Birt' showed that he was the director of a London-based company, and the journalist was able to obtain a front-page scoop by simply investing £4.50 in the Companies House records of Mr Birt's firm. Other individuals who operate in the same way are the spy writers Chapman Pincher and Nigel West (aka Rupert Allason MP) who trade as Summerpage Ltd and Westintel Research Ltd respectively. This is an entirely legal and legitimate practice, but it allows the investigative researcher to obtain considerable background information on these subjects.

Professional registers. Doctors and dentists, solicitors and barristers, accountants and auditors, chartered surveyors and chartered architects, are all professionals who are required to be registered with a professional body, and whose details subsequently appear on the appropriate professional register. These registers are often published – such as the *Medical Register*, *Medical Directory*, *Dentists Register*, *Register of Architects*, *Royal Institution of Chartered Surveyors Yearbook* and many others – and often provide details such as full name, home or business address, professional qualifications, and year of admission to the professional body. Each professional institution and body maintains a central register of their members, and can often supply basic information over the telephone. For example, the United Kingdom Central Council for Nursing, Midwifery and Health Visitors was set up under the Nurses, Midwives and Health Visitors Act 1979, and will confirm details of members over the telephone, but it will not actually offer information. Similarly, the Bar Council registry will provide information about the admission of a barrister to the bar, and details of the chambers from which he or she is currently practising.

Registers of company shareholders. A company must keep a register of its members (shareholders) containing: the name and address of each member; the date that each individual became a shareholder; details of the shares and different classes of shares held by each member; the amount paid or agreed to be paid for those shares; and the date on which any individual ceased to be a member. Companies with 50 or more shareholders must also keep an index of the members, and these details must all be open for public inspection during normal office hours. Details of company directors is also available (see page 96).

School and university records. Personal files held by education authorities are regarded as confidential, and are not normally open to inspection by anyone else. That is why we do not know how many O levels and A levels were gained by the Prime Minister, John Major. A useful source of information about individual former pupils and students can be gleaned from school or college magazines and yearbooks. Officers of the Old Boys or Old Girls associations may be useful leads, as might the public library local to the particular institution. In the case of a college or university, also try the Student Union and, where applicable, the university newspaper or magazine – students can be incredibly resourceful and informative when motivated.

Biography and bibliography. It is possible that your research subject has written a book or had a book written about them. You could begin with the catalogue of your library service, and the library's copy of *Books In Print*. The *Dictionary of National Biography* might be useful, but the most likely source of leads if these fail to produce results is an index of newspaper articles such as *The Humanities Index* and the *Clover Index*. If a review of a book by, or about, your subject has been published in a newspaper, then a reference to that subject will appear in one of these indexes.

Missing persons. A comprehensive and fascinating book on the subjects of missing persons was published in 1986 by Manchester University Press. *Tracing Missing Persons*, by Colin D. Rogers, is a startlingly thorough investigation of almost every department and organization that holds information on anyone – business, commercial, governmental and others. It is a very detailed work, and chiefly of benefit to an investigator attempting to track down someone who wants to be found – such as a long-lost friend or relative. But it is well worth studying and may come up with other sources of information on individuals which could prove useful in a particular case.

Genealogy. This is the study of family trees and the like, but can be a useful process in conducting in-depth research into an individual. A useful starting point is a paperback in the 'Teach Yourself' series, *Trace Your Family History* by L. G. Pine. There is also a *Genealogist's Encyclopedia*, *Genealogist's Guide* and an entire army of professional genealogists represented by the Society of Genealogists. So if you can afford the luxury of paying someone else to undertake the research for you, the society can be contacted at 14 Charterhouse Buildings, London, EC1M 7BA. Telephone 0171–251 8799.

Useful advice on the subject of investigating individuals comes from Carl Bernstein and Bob Woodward, who conducted the fateful investigation into the break-in at the Washington Democrat headquarters which lead to the Watergate scandal. In their book *All The President's Men*, they demonstrate how very basic information on individuals was central to their early investigation. They state: 'The telephone book listed the private security consulting agency run by McCord. There was no answer. They checked the local "criss-cross" directories which listed phone numbers by street addresses. There was no answer at either McCord's home or his business. The address of McCord Associates, 414 Hungerford Drive, Rockville, Maryland, is a large office building, and the cross-reference directory for Rockville lists the tenants.'

Woodward and Bernstein then knocked on a few doors, and spoke to two or three of those tenants. They soon obtained useful background details: 'Gradually, a profile of McCord began to emerge: a native of the Texas panhandle; deeply religious, active in the First Baptist Church of Washington; father of an Air Force cadet and a retarded daughter; ex-FBI agent; military reservist; former chief of physical security for the CIA; teacher of a security course at

Montgomery Junior College; a family man; extremely conscientious; quiet; reliable. John Mitchell's description of McCord notwithstanding, those who knew him agreed that he worked full-time for the President's re-election committee.' As the two intrepid reporters later stated, much of their research was the systematic examination of routine and everyday documents that were in the public domain.

What you can find out about you. There are also a number of legal provisions that allow an individual to access information about themselves, and which at the same time expressly prevent anyone else from doing so.

Data Protection Act 1984. The Data Protection Act regulates the way in which computerized data is used, and allows the data subject (the individual) to obtain print-outs of computer files from the data user (the computer's operator). The rules on disclosure to other parties are very tight, and a range of criminal penalties exists for any breaches of the 1984 Act. The office of the Data Protection Registrar publishes a series of booklets on the workings of the Data Protection Act, and these are well-written and easy to understand. They are available free from the Data Protection Registrar, Wycliffe House, Water Lane, Wilmslow, Cheshire, SK9 5AF. An enquiry line operates on 01625 535777. The National Council for Civil Liberties has published an excellent booklet on the subject, *Data Protection: Putting the Record Straight*, by Roger Cornwell and Marie Staunton, which is available for £4.50 (including postage) from Liberty, 21 Tabard Street, London, SE1 4LA.

Consumer Credit Act 1974. Under this Act, every consumer is entitled to see any credit reference file that is held on them by any credit reference or other agency. If you make an application for credit, whether or not it is refused, you are entitled to ask for the details of the credit reference agency used to check your details. The store or supplier is required in law to give you the information and, in turn, the agency is required to provide you with a copy of your file – whether it is a computer or manual record – for a nominal £1 fee. And you are entitled to have the record put straight if any errors exist. Your local trading standards officer or Citizens Advice Bureau will have more information.

Access to Personal Files Act 1987. This allows for any individual to inspect information held on them by the local authority housing and social services departments. This applies to clients of social services, council tenants and those who have bought or applied to buy their council homes. An individual can inspect and make copies of their files, have mistakes corrected and put a statement on the file over any disputed issue. However, the authority is entitled to charge a fee of up to £10 to cover administrative expenses, and they can refuse to let you see your files if, in their opinion, it might cause you 'serious harm'. This might apply, for example, to a psychiatric patient suffering from a serious psychotic illness.

Access to Medical Reports Act 1988. Individuals have the right of access to medical reports provided by their medical practitioner to insurance companies and employers, and have the right to have inaccurate details corrected. The subject can also withhold consent for the report to be forwarded to the destination insurance company or employer in the event of a dispute.

Chapter five

Companies and Commercial Organizations

MONEY makes the world go round, according to the old song, and it is probably true. It is also true that the protection afforded by limited liability to registered companies is a very attractive benefit to anyone involved in helping money make the world go around: if the company goes bust, the directors and shareholders are protected against the resulting debts. In return for this facility, limited companies and partnerships – of which there are more than 2,500,000 in the UK – are required to place in the public domain a plethora of information on their directors, shareholders, professional advisers (such as auditor and company secretary), trading policy, financing, mortgages, balance sheets, accounts and the like. Therefore, information that is readily available on companies and their directors can be of considerable benefit to investigative researchers.

Here, however, is a list of a number of organizations that are themselves registered as limited companies: The All England Lawn Tennis Club (Wimbledon) Limited; The Bank of England Nominees Limited; St Bartholomew's Hospital (Nominees) Limited; the Campaign for Freedom of Information Limited; Carlton Club Limited; the Church Estates Development and Improvement Company Limited; Joseph Rowntree Reform Trust Limited; the Law Society

Limited; Lloyds of London Limited; the National Union of Mine-workers Limited; the Royal Masonic Benevolent Institution (Services) Limited.

Indeed, charities, friendly societies, voluntary groups, campaigning organizations, trusts, co-operatives, clubs, religious organizations, housing associations, landlords, professional practices (such as doctors and solicitors) – even individuals (see page 85) – can all be limited companies. Given that companies and all these types of organizations exercise considerable power over other people's lives, groups of workers, the environment, even entire communities, then it is worth bearing in mind that money is power (which is true, although it might also sound like a rallying political cry of the now-defunct revolutionary Left). And as it is possible to extract a mountain of information from any of these companies, it is useful to draw up a checklist or strategy outline of the information being sought – as was done in Chapter 4 – and the various sources available to the researcher for undertaking that research. This is because it is important to have a clear idea of precisely what research is to be undertaken, and why this particular information is considered to be of value.

A checklist would include the following:

- What specific information about this or any other company is needed in order to research this subject?

- Is it possible to obtain any or all of the information from existing published sources that are stocked in an accessible public reference library?

- Will it be worthwhile investing a few pounds for a Companies House microfiche of this firm's Companies House records?

- Does this investigation require detailed technical information about the business operations of the company? If so, what time factor and budget has been allocated to locating and collating such information?

- Is there anyone else – such as a pressure group, campaigning organization, trade union or journalist – who

Figure 1: How to trace company information

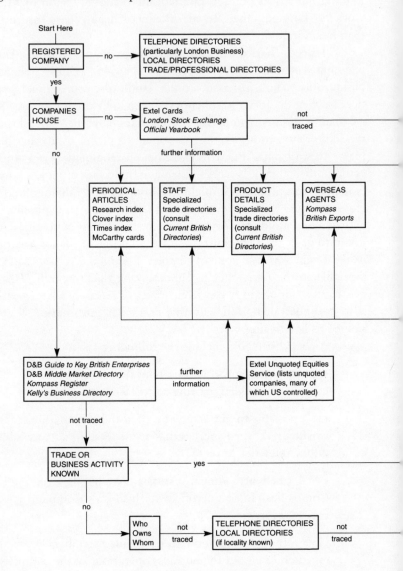

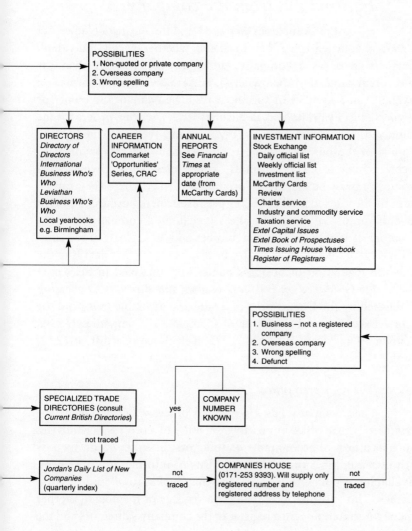

POSSIBILITIES
1. Non-quoted or private company
2. Overseas company
3. Wrong spelling

DIRECTORS
Directory of Directors
International Business Who's Who
Leviathan Business Who's Who
Local yearbooks e.g. Birmingham

CAREER INFORMATION
Commarket 'Opportunities' Series, CRAC

ANNUAL REPORTS
See *Financial Times* at appropriate date (from McCarthy Cards)

INVESTMENT INFORMATION
Stock Exchange
    Daily official list
    Weekly official list
    Investment list
McCarthy Cards
    Review
    Charts service
    Industry and commodity service
    Taxation service
Extel Capital Issues
Extel Book of Prospectuses
Times Issuing House Yearbook
Register of Registrars

POSSIBILITIES
1. Business – not a registered company
2. Overseas company
3. Wrong spelling
4. Defunct

SPECIALIZED TRADE DIRECTORIES (consult *Current British Directories*)

COMPANY NUMBER KNOWN

Jordan's Daily List of New Companies (quarterly index)

COMPANIES HOUSE (0171-253 9393). Will supply only registered number and registered address by telephone

yes

not traced

not traced

not traced

will already have undertaken this or similar research into this company?

Information from the company

Under the Companies Act 1981 and the Business Names Act 1985, anyone carrying out business, whether as an individual, partnership or as a company, under any name other than the individual name(s) of the owner(s), must make certain information available in a number of specific ways. The name of the owner or owners must be printed on all business letters, written orders for the supply of goods and services, invoices and receipts issued in the course of the business, and written demands for the payment of debts arising from the business. The names of the owners of a company must be displayed 'prominently' (i.e. where they can be seen by the visiting public) on *any* premises where business is carried out. If the owner of the business is a limited company then the Companies House registration number and the address of the company's registered office must also be displayed. Further details of the use and regulation of business names are contained in the leaflet *Notes for Guidance on Business Names and Business Ownership* published by the Department of Trade and available free from the Chief Executive and Registrar of Companies, Companies House, Crown Way, Cardiff, CF4 3UZ. Telephone Cardiff (01222) 38036.

The registered office

Each company has a registered office, which might be the company's head office or possibly the office of a professional adviser such as a firm of accountants or solicitors. In either event, the law requires a number of registers and lists of information to be kept, available for public inspection, and that applies to *all* limited companies. This information includes: a register of members (another name for shareholders); a register of the company's directors and the company secretary; a register of mortgages and charges (that means debts and loans that are formally secured against the property and/or assets of the company); a register of debenture holders; a register of the directors' interests in shares and debentures; an index of shareholders who hold more than five per cent of the company's shares; copies of the directors' contracts of service; and the minutes of general company meetings. These provisions are required in law under various sections of the Companies Act 1985, and if a company fails to comply with a request for this information – and members of the public making a request for such information from a company are not required to state *why* they want it or who they are – then it can be reported to the Companies Investigations Branch of the Department of Trade and Industry, Ashdown House, 123 Victoria Street, London, SW1E 6RB. Telephone 0171–215 6525. They publish a very informative brochure entitled *Investigations – How They Work* which is available without charge from that address.

Companies House records

A set of microfiches containing all the documents held on a company at Companies House is available to the public for a fee of £4.50. This is remarkably good value if a researcher is carrying out an investigation on a specific company. However, there are several considerations that might complicate matters. The first is that the researcher has either to go along to one of the Companies House offices – they are located in Cardiff, London, Edinburgh and Belfast, with additional satellite offices in Leeds, Manchester and Birmingham – or to undertake a postal search. A postal search costs (at current prices) £5.50 including the search fee and first-class return postage. If undertaking a postal search then it is advisable to call Companies House to confirm the rates that apply at the time. The numbers for the Postal Search Services are: Cardiff (01222) 380801; Edinburgh 0131–225 5774; and Belfast (01232) 2344488, and they accept payment credit and debit cards. Another complication is that a company might be a subsidiary of a parent or holding company, and may indeed be one of several or even dozens of such subsidiaries. In that case it will be necessary to conduct some preliminary research at the company's registered office, or through one of the numerous company information directories listed below, so as to narrow down the field to the appropriate subsidiary. Otherwise one might be left holding a number of unhelpful and costly bundles of Companies House microfiches.

The information that appears on the Companies House microfiche includes: address of the registered office; the full name, home address, date of birth, nationality, occupation and other directorships of each of the company's directors and the company secretary; a summary of the issued share capital (this gives an indication of the company's operating wealth); a list of past and present shareholders, including names, addresses, number and types of shares held, dates of purchase and disposal; amount and size of debts secured by the company in the form of mortgages and other charges against the company's assets; copies of the annual accounts and balance sheets; a certified copy of the auditor's annual report; a copy of the articles and memorandum of association (which are the company's governing documents and which should reveal the nature of the company's trade). And all these documents are historical and cumulative – in other words, the microfiche will contain both the most up-to-date versions of those documents, and all previous documents filed since the company was formed. The records will also contain all official documents relating to the winding-up, receivership or liquidation of a company that goes out of business.

Directories

There are a number of invaluable directories and other sources of information on companies that are stocked by reference libraries, and which could supply the information needed for an investigation. The following are indispensable sources that are often stocked by main reference libraries.

The Stock Exchange Yearbook. This gem is published by Macmillan and costs £210 for 932 pages in 1994/95 – and each page is packed with useful information on some 4,000 major companies listed on the London and Dublin Stock Exchanges, plus those traded on the Unlisted Securities Market. The entries provide information on: registered office; directors and company secretary; principal subsidiaries; company history and activities; balance sheet details; capital; loans; auditors; solicitors; bankers; etc. It also provides information on major companies in liquidation, administration and receivership; overseas stock exchanges; corporation and county council stocks; home and overseas government bonds; a register of 'defunct and other companies'; a list of stockbrokers trading on the London Stock Exchange; and details of the membership of the Board of the London Stock Exchange.

Directory of Directors. This two-volume directory cross-references companies with their directors, and lists directors and their companies. Volume 1 lists 75,000 company directors and board members, and the companies of which they are directors. Volume 2 lists some 15,000 British companies and gives details of each one's directors and subsidiaries, if any. It also provides a three-year history of turnover, profit before tax, fixed asset value, current assets and liabilities, and shareholder funds and assets employed by the company.

Who Owns Whom. This is a useful two-volume directory for sorting out the tangle of parent companies and their subsidiaries. The first volume lists some 7,000 parent companies under which is a further list of all the company's subsidiaries; the second volume lists all the subsidiary companies in alphabetical order, of which there are more than 100,000, and then matches them with their parent company.

Key British Enterprises (Dun and Bradstreet). This is a huge six-volume work totalling some 7,000 pages of data on Britain's biggest 50,000 companies and is divided into several categories. It provides contact details: name of company contact and office address; telephone, fax and telex numbers; names and functions of directors. Financial details: authorized capital; issued capital; sales turnover; export sales turnover; profit figures; auditors. Operational details: line of business; markets; trade names; number of employees; location of branches. Corporate details: parent company; date established; legal status; company registration number; VAT number; bankers; trade awards; Royal Warrants held. Volumes 1–3 provide an alphabetical list of the companies; volume 4 provides industrial and geographical cross-references; volume 5 covers trade names, export markets and directors details; and volume 6 provides listings of Dun and Bradstreet's renowned 'British Business Rankings' – a form of company credit scoring.

Kompass. This is another huge three-volume publication from Reed Information Services which describes itself as 'The authority on British industry' and is published in association with the Confederation of British Industry (CBI). Volume 1 includes details of some 41,000 different products and services provided by the companies listed in the other sections. Volume 2 details corporate information on 43,500 leading industrial companies. This data includes: details of 100,000 parent companies and their subsidiaries; details of their corporate structure; details of the 100,000 registered trade names and 16,000 lapsed trade names of 25,000 industrial concerns; and details of the 'quality assessments achieved' by some 13,000 of the bigger companies. Volume 1 also provides a detailed profile of the inside working of the Confederation of British Industries including objectives, membership, council, standing committees and their chairmen (*sic*), organizational structure, and regional offices. These volumes contain some 6,000 pages of invaluable information on British industry.

Sells Product and Services Directory. This slightly more modest two-volume annual is divided into three main sections covering some 50,000 companies: a products and services section; a brand and trade names section; and a section on company data. The company data section provides brief outline information on the company, including: address of head office; number of employees; and the names of the managing director and company secretary.

Kelly's Business Directory. This directory from the Reed Information Group is effectively a glorified Yellow Pages telephone directory covering the whole of the UK and listing the details of some 82,000 industrial product and services companies. The data is primarily aimed at business people looking for sources of raw materials, manufactured goods and industrial services.

Macmillan's Unquoted Companies. This provides details of smaller companies that are not quoted on the London Stock Exchange. It includes a financial profile of Britain's top 20,000 unquoted companies whose annual turnover exceeds £4.9 million. The information given covers key company, personnel and parent company details. It also includes a variety of industry league tables and cross-referenced indexes.

The Price Waterhouse Corporate Register. 'The number 1 information source on decision-makers in UK Stock Market companies', according to the register's blurb. This is a valuable guide to the tens of thousands of directors and office-holders in thousands of UK companies. The first part of the register lists the companies in alphabetical order, including details of the registered office, capital, executive directors, non-executive directors, company secretary, directors' pay, number of employees, brokers, auditors, bankers and solicitors. The second part is a *Who's Who* of all directors and office-holders listed in the first part, giving details of the names, addresses and telephone numbers for 20,000 key directors, executives and professional advisers; directors' shareholdings (ordinary and incentive shares), a list of all companies, professional bodies and institutes with which they are connected; directors' and executives' career histories and current job titles, and details of their personal background including date of birth, education, club membership, marital and family details and other interests; and company secretary's name. Earlier editions of this publication were called the Arthur Anderson Corporate Register. Four fully updated editions of this directory are published every year.

The Hambro Company Guide. This has similarities to the Price Waterhouse Corporate Register, and provides a range of background financial data on thousands of British companies. But it also has a particularly useful section listing the corporate clients of the top names in auditing, financial advice, public relations, foreign banks, investment managers, international lawyers, property advisers, registrars, solicitors and stockbrokers.

Jordans – Britain's Top Privately Owned Companies. A five-volume directory which alphabetically lists the details of company address, nature of business, name of chief executive, and telephone number. It also includes a classification of the companies by industry and geographical groupings. Volume 5 additionally includes a complete index of all 10,000 companies.

The Guardian Guide to the UK's Top Companies. This is a helpful guide that provides detailed information on corporate structures, trading performances and share price fluctuations of the companies listed. It also provides a profile of each company's 'corporate conscience' reflecting its attitude to ethical issues at a policy and practical level.

Extel Cards. Some public library services will subscribe to the Extel Card service, which are stored in distinctive small metal filing cabinets. The cards detail information on more than 6,000 companies which matches, and sometimes even surpasses, the information available from Companies House, but they contain a copyright warning that the material must not be photocopied. And some librarians are particularly committed to enforcing copyright. So researchers are strongly advised against any intended plans to sneakily photocopy this highly useful material when the coast is clear.

McCarthy Cards. This is a similar system in style to the Extel Cards which monitors the press coverage on more than 3,000 UK companies in more than 70 newspapers and financial periodicals. The articles are reduced in size by photocopying and stored in a manual filing system that is regularly updated.

Annual reports. Most major companies publish a glossy annual report which serves two purposes: it fulfils a range of statutory requirements under the Companies Acts in reporting information to shareholders and others; and it can serve as a useful public relations tool in promoting the company and its image generally. But annual reports are also a useful source of intelligence on companies, and will at least set out the following information: a summons to the annual general meeting; the directors' and chairman's annual report; the company's balance sheet and profit-and-loss accounts; details of parent, associated and subsidiary companies; and the auditor's report. They can also contain a wide range of useful and interesting facts. One such, by way of example, is the annual report and accounts of the Church Commissioner for England. Although the Church of England is a well-known and established religious organization, it is also a multimillion pound business enterprise in the form of the Church Commissioners. Their annual report shows, for example, that they own 100 per cent of the following companies: Cricklewood Estates (Investments) Limited; Ickham Gravel Limited; Paternoster Development Limited (in liquidation); CC Projects Limited (CC is an abreviation for Church

Commissioners); CC Property Investments Incorporated; Elmswood Limited; and Deansbank Properties Incorporated. The report also details the Church Commissioners holdings of hundreds of millions of shares in hundreds of companies both in the UK and abroad, and numerous commercial property holdings such as: the Metro Centre, Gateshead (valued at over £20 m); the Angel Centre, Islington, London, EC1 (similarly valued at over £20 m); the Spitfire Trading Estate, Heston (valued at between £3 m and £5 m); and so on. Annual reports can be a real eye-opener and a major source of information on the larger companies.

Trade directories. There are specialist trade directories for every occasion. The *Bankers Almanac and Yearbook* provides a detailed profile of 3,600 major clearing banks and merchant banks trading in this country, and details their history, directors, executives, regional directors, overseas subsidiaries and branches. The *Building Societies Yearbook* lists every building society in the UK and provides information on their directors, executives, head office, year of incorporation and number of branches. The *Insurance Directory and Yearbook* is a 2,000 page annual that provides a wealth of inside details on insurance companies, brokers, the ill-fated Lloyds syndicates, statistics and a *Who's Who* of key individuals. It is likely that there is a trade directory of some description on every conceivable subject. The main trade directories are listed in *Current British Directories*, and a thorough range of trade information – both printed and on-line – is kept by the British Library's Science Reference and Information Service (with more than 215,000 reference books and 60,000 specialist journal titles on the shelves). This gold-mine of information is based in central London and is open to the public. They publish a range of guides to their services, and their Business information Service can be contacted on 0171–323–7454 during normal office hours. Their address is 25 Southampton Buildings, London, WC2A 1AW.

There are numerous other publications on company information that appear on library shelves and which are not listed here. The crucial thing is to become familiar with the data contained in the publications to which you have access, and perhaps to take the opportunity of visiting the nearest major reference library to your location and make a note for future reference of the major titles that are stocked.

Company research and information services

The researcher with unlimited financial resources, or the media organization with a major commitment to investigative journalism, might benefit from the services provided by some of the large financial information publishers. Here is an outline of the services available from the six biggest business information services (in alphabetical order) from whom brochures and promotional material can be freely obtained.

Dun and Bradstreet International. Their Business Reference Services covers a range of international business directories relating to almost every part of the globe; a range of specialist business directories relating to the UK (such as *Key British Enterprises* and *Who Owns Whom*); and an on-line business information service that it describes as 'The ultimate UK business database'. This provides the type of information that appears on the Companies House records, together with more detailed market and trade information on some 50,000 British companies. Dun and Bradstreet also publish an interesting range of regional directories containing company information on local and regional businesses. Details of all these service are available from Dun and Bradstreet International, Holmers Farm Way, High Wycombe, Buckinghamshire, HP12 4UL. Telephone: (01494) 422000.

The Economist Intelligence Unit. From the publishers of *The Economist* comes a 70-page catalogue detailing the range of business information services available from this major group. Its publications include *Country Reports*, *Country Profiles*, *World Outlook*, *Country Forecasts*, *Country Risk Service*, *Investing, Licensing and Trade Conditions Abroad*, *Financing Foreign Operations*, *Crossborder and Crossborder Monitor*, and *Market Access*. It publishes a range of research reports on specific industries, such as *Threats to Copper Supply: A Political Risk Analysis*, *Investing in Eastern Europe and Russia*, and *Tax Havens and Their Uses*. It is are based at 40 Duke Street, London, W1A 1DW. Telephone 0171–830 1000.

Extel Financial Limited. The publishers of the Extel Cards describe themselves, as 'the definitive centre for financial and corporate information'. They operate a financial intelligence service covering 25,000 annual company reports and accounts, 120,000 international equities, marketing data on 80 countries, etc. This information can be supplied in printed form or on a range of computerized systems. They have records on British companies that go back to 1965 and publish a range of business handbooks. They are located at: Extel Financial Limited, Fitzroy House, 13–17 Epworth Street, London, EC2A 4DL. Telephone: 0171–251 3333.

FT Business Information. This service comes from the publishers of the *Financial Times* newspaper, and covers a range of services from one-off reports to on-line databases, newswires, telephone and fax services – in fact, all the facilities needed to transform the humble researcher into a City dealer. The FT runs the FT Business Research Centre, which accesses the FT library; over 1,000 on-line databases; all directories, reports and trade and industry press; and an extensive range of personal contacts. Its promotional material states that its clients' queries range '... from the very simple, like a request for a copy of a company's annual report, to complex marketing questions such as requests to investigate the emergence of the trade marketing manager within the retail manufacturing industry'. It continues: 'FT Business Research Centre is the UK's leading information broker, providing on-demand business information covering a wide range of topics including companies, industries and markets, statistics, personalities and current affairs.' One specific service offered is 'FT Media Intelligence – a no-frills service for the print and broadcast industry which offers fast turnaround of press clippings, database sweeps and transcripts to high-volume users.' A word of warning about the costs: the minimum 'annual commitment' is £2,000, and the applicable hourly research rate is £70.00. But its catalogue is well worth looking at, and the main FT Business Information Office is located at Number One, Southwark Bridge, London, SE1 9HL. Telephone: 0171–873 3000.

Jordans. Jordan and Sons Limited is an established publishing company producing a range of annual reports on specific industries and areas of business that detail the top players in that business, their turnovers, market share, and other statistical data. For example, they publish *Britain's Top 500 Defence Companies*, *Britain' Security Industry*, *Britain's Top Privately Owned Companies* (volumes 1–5), and *Britain's Waste Management Industry*. A copy of its complete list of published titles is available from Sales Department, Jordan and Sons Limited, Freepost (BS2348), PO Box 260, Bristol, BS99 7XZ.

McCarthy Information Services. McCarthy publishes a range of hard-copy, microfiche and on-line business information including the *McCarthy Cards*. The information is extracted from more than 70 of the world's leading newspapers and magazines, and covers: unit trusts; share prices; foreign exchanges; the money markets; commodities; London Traded Options; Base Lending Rates; and so on. It also operates MIRAC which is a data collection and distribution service specializing in company reports and accounts. One particularly useful service provided by McCarthy is its Unquoted Company Service, which includes companies that do not have an Ordinary Share Quotation on the Stock Market such as private and government-controlled organizations, plus companies from many parts of the world not included elsewhere. They are at: Unit 10, Old Silk Works, Beech Avenue, Warminster, Wiltshire, BA12 8LX. Telephone (01985) 215151.

Specialist advice

There are a number of voluntary-sector and quasi-commercial organizations that have a specialist knowledge of researching companies and commercial concerns. They may be able to help in a particular case, and if so would be far less costly than the main business information groups listed above.

Labour Research Department. This an independent trade union research body that is not part of the Labour Party, but which has its roots in the labour and trade union movements. It describes itself as: ' ... providing trade unionists with the information they need for: collective bargaining; promoting equal opportunities; campaigning against cuts; assessing workplace hazards; fighting privatisation; knowing their employment rights; benefit claims; and much, much more.' LRD publishes *Labour Research* magazine;

Bargaining Report; Fact Service; and *LRD Booklets.* It also operates an enquiry service for affiliated organizations which has advised on such matters as comparative pay, MPs' interests, health and safety issues, political donations by companies, and the like. Additionally it provides a Company Enquiry Service which is simply obtaining the Companies House records for much the same price as a postal search directly to Companies House. The Labour Reseach Department is seen as the expert in researching political donations, and the funding of political parties and other such organizations as the British United Industrialists and Aims of Industry. Affiliation fees start at £48.25 for local political parties and trade councils, and the annual subscription rate for the Fact Service is £44.00. The LRD is at 78 Blackfriars Road, London, SE1 8HF. Telephone 0171–928 3649.

EIRIS – the Ethical Investment Research Service. EIRIS was set up by a group of churches and charities in 1983 to establish a database of all major UK listed companies and groups. This is to provide an ethical 'check-up' on companies for investors and others concerned about ethical investment. A free leaflet on information services EIRIS can provide to help individual investors concerned about ethical issues is available from EIRIS Services Limited at 504 Bondway Business Centre, 71 Bondway, London, SW8 1SQ. Telephone 0171–735 1351.

CAITS – Centre for Alternative Industrial and Technological Systems. This is an alternative research body founded by the Lucas Aerospace Shop Stewards Committee in 1978 to develop the committee's Workers Alternative Plan – to replace redundancy and unemployment with socially useful work. It has since been engaged to undertake 'labour market and corporate investigations' for a number of local government authorities around the country. Further details of the organization's work, publications and courses is available from its office at 404 Camden Road, London, N7 0SJ. Telephone 0171–607 7079.

Investigatory and regulatory bodies

The following is an outline of a number of official bodies that have a duty to investigate aspects of companies' activities.

Department of Trade and Industry Investigations Division.
The Secretary of State for Trade and Industry (also known as the
President of the Board of Trade) has legal powers to investigate
misconduct and fraud in commercial enterprises. These laws are set
down mainly in the Companies Acts of 1985 and 1989, and are
summarized here. COMPANIES ACT 1985, SECTION 432: The
Secretary of State is empowered to appoint inspectors to investigate
the affairs of a company. This usually happens if there is a suspicion
of fraud, misconduct or the withholding from shareholders of
information about the company's activities and performance to
which they are entitled. The courts also have power to require
inspectors to be appointed. COMPANIES ACT 1985, SECTION
442: This allows the Secretary of State to appoint inspectors to
investigate the ownership of a company, as companies have a legal
right to know who owns their shares. The Department states that
'The Secretary of State always announces the appointment of inspectors. Their reports are usually published if there is a public interest
.... . There are cases in which there is little or no interest in a
published report.' COMPANIES ACT 1985, SECTION 446: This
empowers the Secretary of State to launch an investigation into
share dealings by company directors and their families in their own
companies or associate companies. This particularly relates to illegal
dealing in share options or the failure by a director to declare an
interest in a company that she or he controls. COMPANIES ACT
1985, SECTION 447: Most company investigations are carried out
under this section, which can require a company to produce its
records, such as accounts books, ledgers, and other documentation.
Under this section the Secretary of State has power to authorize the
seizure of papers. COMPANIES ACT 1989, SECTION 82: This
gives the Secretary of State wide powers to assist an overseas
regulatory body conduct an investigation into a British-based company. FINANCIAL SERVICES ACT 1986: SECTION 105 provides
the Secretary of State with powers to investigate investment businesses normally regulated by the self-regulatory organizations;
SECTION 94 provides the same powers to investigate unit trusts;
SECTION 177 relates to powers to investigate insider dealing. A
copy of the booklet *Investigations – How They Work* is available

from the DTI Investigations Division, Ashdown House, 123 Victoria Street, London, SW1E 6RB. Telephone: 0171-215 6525. For a case study of the application of these laws and the release of investigatory information, it is worth looking at press clippings relating to a DTI investigation into share dealings by Lord Archer in the summer of 1994.

Office of Fair Trading. The Annual Report of the Director General of Fair Trading is a fascinating read, as its 75 pages are a catalogue of unscrupulous and sometimes illegal business activities. The OFT has various legal powers to investigate business dealings – such as those contained in the Consumer Credit Act 1974 and the Estate Agents Act 1979. It also covers competition policy, and turns up a few prospective investigative leads. For example, a paragraph headed 'Cartels' reads: 'The Division sustained its campaign against secret, and therefore unlawful, cartels. No fewer than 50 new investigations were launched in 1992. The major investigation of ready-mixed concrete continues throughout the year ... While the Court of Appeal judgement in the Bicester case is proving a lesser inhibition than had been feared, the concrete cases do illustrate the cumbersome procedures involved in the Restrictive Trade Practices Act and the disadvantages of the Office's limited investigatory powers.' Interesting. The OFT also operates a number of public registers as required in law: the Resgister of Restrictive Trading Agreements, the Consumer Credit Public Register and the Estate Agents Act Public Register. They can be inspected between 10.30 a.m. and 4.30 p.m. during the working week at: The Office of Fair Trading, Consumer Credit Licensing Branch, Government Building, Bromyard Avenue, Acton, London, W3 7BB. It is advisable to telephone first on 0171-242 2858 asking for extention 8900.

Monopolies and Mergers Commission. The Monopolies and Mergers Commission was attacked by the Consumers' Association in July of 1994 as being a 'toothless watchdog' and 'a friend of big business' which, of course, could be true. But the annual review (as its annual report is called) does throw up a few useful titbits for the investigative researcher – including an outline of every case that the Commission investigates. One such case, the provision of bus services in Mid and West Kent, subsequently attracted a considerable amount of press coverage in the quality financial press. So there is the prospect of obtaining some kind of investigative lead and developing a story from the information published by this 'toothless watchdog'.

Chapter six

Local Government

LOCAL government authorities in the UK spend nearly £50 billion every year on the range of services provided by our town and county halls. That is a staggering sum of money, and it has been shown that local government is vulnerable to corruption and maladministration on a big scale. It has also been alleged that local authorities, particularly in inner-city areas, are used by political activists for their own personal gain and career development. Whatever the truth in these allegations, it is a fact that local government provides the public with a range of essential services at a very local level, and should be subject to thorough scrutiny by the local press and public. However, events such as the Poulson corruption case in the 1960s and the Poll Tax débâcle of the late 1980s, show just how important local government is in the UK, and just how controversial it can become.

It would be useful to take a look at examples of different types of local government authority in this country, and remind ourselves of precisely what services they provide and at what cost.

A metropolitan authority – Leeds. A metropolitan authority is a single unitary body responsible for providing all council services in its area. These are the services provided by Leeds Metropolitan Council in 1994/95:

7,600 acres of parks and open spaces
1 airport
3 art galleries
11 public halls
4 museums

18 baths and swimming pools
1 civic theatre
22 cemeteries
3 crematoria
23 children's homes
15 community centres
79,607 council flats and houses
42 day centres
34 family nursery centres
6 golf courses
72 libraries
7 markets
55 residential homes
308 schools

Its income for that period was £508.4 m made up of £258.4 m. from central government; £141 m from business rates; and £109 m from the council tax. That money was spent as follows:

Education   £275.6 m
Social services   £97.5 m
Highways   £33.1 m
Recreation/tourism   £27.9 m
Passenger transport   £23.9 m
Refuse collection   £13.8 m
Housing   £10.4 m
Planning/economic development   £7.9
Contingencies   £2.3 m
Other   £16.0 m

A district council – Cheltenham. District councils have no responsibility for education, social services and only partial responsibility for planning (these services being provided by county councils). This is Cheltenham's service provision for 1993/94:

643 acres of parks and open spaces
6,378 council flats and houses
1 airport
1 art gallery
1 athletics stadium

2 baths and pools
2 cemeteries
1 crematorium
2 civic theatres
1 market
1 museum

Its income for that financial year totalled £43.1 m, made up of £10.7 m from central government; £17.7 m from rent and charges; £9.9 m from the council tax; £2.2 m from interest payments; and £2.6 m from other sources. It was spent in the following ways:

Council housing   £14.0 m
Housing benefits   £6.6 m
Financing costs   £5.0 m
Environmental health   £4.3 m
Leisure/recreation   £4.1 m
Highways/car parking   £3.6 m
Other   £3.8 m
Community charge write-off   £1.7 m

London – the London borough of Ealing. London boroughs are unitary authorities but have no responsibility for police and public transport services. In 1994/95 LB Ealing provided the following services and facilities:

1,900 acres of parks and open spaces
17,984 council flats and houses
3 advice and information centres
20 car parks
5 cemeteries
5 children's homes
4 Further Education colleges
5 homes for the mentally ill/learning difficulties
12 libraries
2 museums
9 homes for the aged
9 play centres
3 public halls
95 schools and nursery centres

10 sports and leisure centres
5 swimming pools
20 youth and community centres

Its income for 1994/95 was £249 m, made up of £145.2 m in central government grants; £56 m from business rates; £13.7 m from a special government grant; and £34.1 m from the council tax. Its spending that year was:

Education   £112.3 m
Social services   £46.0 m
Highways   £8.4 m
Planning   £3.4 m
Recreation   £18.0 m
Environmental health   £4.8 m
Refuse collection   £9.7 m
Housing   £9.1 m
Other services   £24.0 m
Contingencies/levies   £13.3 m

So, local government is big business. And this multimillion pound big business affects everyone's lives, and operates right under our noses. And we all pay for it too, so there are a number of valid reasons for keeping local government under check and ensuring that our elected representatives are behaving themselves, especially as they often do not behave quite as they should.

A survey of London local government undertaken in January 1992 by the *Independent* newspaper revealed the following shocking details of fraud and corruption investigations being carried out at the time (all details correct at the time of the survey being undertaken). BARNET: Conservative-controlled. Inquiries: theft and deception; two former staff convicted. BRENT: Conservative-controlled with support of independent Democrat Labour councillors. Inquiries: Public Sector Corruption Unit investigation, council flats keys for sale; 11 arrests, including councillors and housing officers. BROMLEY: Conservative-controlled. Inquiries: Public Sector Corruption Unit inquiry into two allegations – one corruption, and one fraud and corruption; eight arrests. CAMDEN: Labour-controlled. Inquiries: housing benefit fraud and keys-for-sale; one employee sacked; two convicted – one for housing benefit fraud, one for collusion. ENFIELD: Conservative-controlled. Inquiry: Public Sector Corruption Unit investigation awaiting court proceedings. GREENWICH: Labour-controlled. Inquiries: two fraud squad investigations into keys-for-sale, housing benefits and Right to Buy frauds. HACKNEY: Labour-controlled. Inquiries: six Public Sector Corruption Unit fraud and corruption investigations into housing benefit and keys-for-sale fraud, possibly involving an illegal immigrant racket. Council investigating 75 'irregularities'; one conviction for theft and conspiracy to pervert the course of justice; 17 staff sacked; 22 arrests, 13 charged with fraud and theft – nine of whom were former staff members. HAMMERSMITH AND FULHAM: Labour-controlled. Inquiries: keys-for-sale; housing benefit investigation; fraud squad investigating alleged corruption in engineering department; 11 staff suspended; eight housing benefit prosecutions. HARINGEY: Labour-controlled. Inquiries: two Public Sector Corruption Unit investigations into housing benefit fraud. HOUNSLOW: Labour-controlled. Inquiry: Right to Buy fraud. ISLINGTON: Labour-controlled. Inquiries: one Public Sector Corruption Unit investigation and internal inquiry into allegations of bribe-taking by street market inspectors; one sacked and appealing. KENSINGTON AND CHELSEA: Conservative-controlled. Inquiries: housing benefit fraud; eight prosecutions. LAMBETH: Labour-controlled. Inquiries: six Public Sector Corruption Unit inquiries; Brixton police prosecution in housing benefit fraud; three council officers suspended and charged. LEWISHAM: Labour-controlled. Inquiries: housing benefit fraud; keys-for-sale investigation; one officer sacked. SOUTHWARK: Labour-controlled. Inquiries: one Public Sector Corruption Unit corruption inquiry; internal and District Auditor investigating; one arrest. TOWER HAMLETS: Liberal Democrat-controlled. Inquiries: four Public Sector Corruption Unit investigations – three corruption and one failure to declare an interest; street market bribery, keys-for-sale and housing benefit fraud; three prosecutions and two housing officers sacked. WALTHAM FOREST: Labour-controlled. Inquiries: allegations of fraud and other irregularities led to 28 prosecutions. WANDSWORTH: Conservative-controlled. Inquiries; housing benefit fraud. WESTMINSTER: Conservative-controlled. Inquiries: one Public Sector Corruption Unit fraud inquiry; District Auditor investigation; Charity Commission investigating; one conviction for theft.

That is a rather disturbing snapshot of criminal and internal investigations in London's local government at one given time. And there is nothing especially unusual about those levels of doubt and uncertainty in local government. Therefore, there is wide scope for investigative reseach in the field of local government. What is particularly disturbing about this level of corruption is that local government is one area of official life that has the benefit of a Freedom of Information Act called the Local Government (Access to Information) Act 1985. This is the key to an in-depth public investigation of local government in Britain. But first a look at some more basic research material.

The single most useful source of basic information about any local government authority in the UK is the *Municipal Yearbook* which comes in two volumes, contains more than 2,000 pages and covers every local authority in the country. It lists all the detailed information about the range of services provided by each authority; all the principal council officers; the names and addresses of all the elected councillors; and the names of all the council committee chairpersons. There is a separate section on each area of local authority activity – such as waste disposal, environmental health, social services and housing – and details of professional associations and specialist bodies working in those particular spheres. It also provides a useful list of all local public officials such as Lords Lieutenant, High Sheriffs and coroners. The complexities of local government in London following the demise of the Greater London Council and Inner London Education Authority are clearly detailed. Information on MPs, MEPs, central government departments, regulatory bodies, development corporations, and the like are also listed. This should be regarded as the Bible of local government, and most libraries with a reference section will have a copy – or ask at the town hall.

Although the Local Government (Access to Information) Act 1985 allows the public to obtain a wide range of information on local councils, there are often problems with councils refusing to comply fully with these requirements – which we shall examine later in this chapter. There is one avenue open to a member of the public who is encountering obstructive council officials or wanting to obtain detailed or internal documents to which even the 1985 Act would not allow access. The one essential requirement for this route, however, is a friendly and co-operative councillor who is prepared to make a personal application to the council for the information.

Individual councillors have wide legal rights of access to council documentation that extends far beyond any of the rights under the Local Government (Access to Information) Act 1985. The legal precedent for this exists in a fairly straightforward High Court case that was heard in 1983 called the case of Birmingham City Council versus O (O is the initial of a child in the care of Birmingham council's social services department). The case's reference numbers, which will be needed for looking up a record of the judgement in the law books, are: 1983 A.C.579; and 1983 1 All E.R.497.

The case related to a councillor who was a member of the council's social services committee and was concerned about the treatment of a child in council care. She requested to see the personal case file on the child, but council officers refused her access to this sensitive information because, they claimed, the law would not extend to providing a councillor with such detailed and personal material. The councillor was not satisfied with the rebuttal, and made an application to the High Court for judicial review (which simply means asking the High Court to interpret the law in a particular case).

In his summing up, Lord Brightman gave an explicit judgement: 'In the case of a committee of which he (*sic*) is a member, a councillor as a general rule will *ex hypothesi* have good reason for access to all written material of such a committee. So I do not doubt that each member of the social services committee is entitled by virtue of his office to see all the papers which have come into the possession of a social worker in the course of his duties as an employee of the council. There is no room for any secrecy between a social worker and a member of the social services committee.'

Thus, in the case of a committee of which a councillor is a member, that councillor has the legal right of access to *all* documents relating to all aspects of the work of that committee and its corresponding council department. This applies even to aspects of the council's business that might not be dealt with by the committee itself – business carried out by delegation to officers, or simply handled as day-to-day management or operational tasks. Therefore, in a major enquiry or investigation, it is possible for a journalist, campaigner or local resident to ask a councillor to obtain detailed inside information. And, according to this case law, the council is obliged to provide that information. It does not follow, incidentally, that a councillor has the legal right to *disclose* all such material that is obtained in this way to any other person. The councillor will be under a 'common law' legal duty to maintain the confidentiality of much internal council material – especially if it refers to a child in the care of the social services. But in the case of the councillor uncovering, say, a case of corruption in the award of a council contract, then there would also be a strong case that the councillor should blow the whistle. We shall look in some more detail later on about using these types of obscure tactic to obtain information where a council is being obstructive.

Local Government (Access to Information) Act 1985

The rights contained in the Local Government (Access to Information) Act 1985 can be summarized as follows:

• The press and public have a legal right to attend meetings of the council and of its committees and sub-committees that make decisions on behalf of the council. This provision applies to any decision-making body of the council whatever it might be called (such as working parties, advisory groups or consultative committees) if they have decision-making powers (Sections 100A and 100E).

• A council notice announcing the date, time and place of all such meetings must be displayed in a public place at least three clear working days before the meeting takes place (Sections 100A(6) and 100E).

• In advance of such meetings taking place, the press and public must be allowed access to the agenda, reports and relevant background internal documents. These must be available for inspection at the council's offices at least three days in advance of meetings (Sections 100B, 100D and 100E).

• Copies of the minutes of previous meetings of the council, its committees and sub-committees and other decision-making bodies of the council must be available for public inspection for a minimum period of six years (Section 100C).

• All council agenda and reports relating to council meetings must also be available for public inspection for the subsequent six years. All relevant internal council documents used at council meetings must be available for four years (Sections 100C and 100D).

• If the press and public are excluded from a council meeting in order for confidential business to be discussed, then they can be excluded only by a resolution of the meeting. There is no facility for a presumption that only 'excluded' business will be discussed. The presumption has to be the other way – that the public has the right to attend even if only to hear a resolution to have them excluded. That way, at least the public knows what committees and sub-committees exist, and when they meet (Sections 100A, 100C and Schedule 12A.

• The council has to make available for public inspection at its main offices a list of the names and addresses of all council members (councillors) and details of the membership of all its committees and sub-committees (Section 100G).

• If a council officer is given 'delegated authority' by the council to take decisions on its behalf, then a public register must provide details of the council officer and the precise details of those delegated powers (Section 100G).

• The council must provide for public inspection at its main office a summary of the public rights of access to council meetings and documents under the Local Government (Access to Information) Act 1985. This must be available for inspection during normal office hours (Section 100G).

• Members of the public may be required to pay a 'reasonable fee' to inspect internal documents – but not to inspect the agendas, minutes or reports (although the Act does not define the meaning of the term 'reasonable') (Section 100H).

• The council must make photocopy facilities available for anyone wishing to copy any of the council documents that they have the right to inspect. Again, the council may charge a 'reasonable' fee for the use of such facilities (Section 100H).

• These rights apply to all other local government bodies such as a Police Authority or joint committee of two or more local government authorities (Section 100J).

Anyone who plans to use these provisions is advised to obtain a copy of the Local Government (Access to Information) Act 1985, so that it can be produced during discussions with officials about its application. Because although it appears here that local government benefits from a Freedom of Information Act, there is a body of evidence that suggests widespread non-compliance with the Act. For example, South Herefordshire District Council stated in a report that certain details of the council's activities are kept confidential 'because of the sensitivity of the information being transacted'. This applied to business conducted by the Public Conveniences Advisory Group and the Dogs and Litter Advisory Group. And Ogwr Borough Council in Wales stated that one of its sub-committees does not comply with the provisions of the 1985 Act because of 'commercial confidentiality'. And the name of this body? It was the Pantomime Sub-committee of course. So, it is one thing to have the law on the statute book; it is another, however, to make that law work.

Making the law work

According to surveys undertaken by campaigners for more public access to local government information, a large minority of local government authorities around the country fail to comply fully with the Local Government (Access to Information) Act 1985. They can do this because the government leaves it to the individual authorities to police themselves in this respect. And local government officers can be most imaginative in the way they interpret the 1985 Act.

Here is a typical example of a local government officer obstructing a researcher attempting to obtain information about the award of a controversial contract by the council. The researcher will contact the authority specifying the detailed information that s/he would like to see. Let us say that it refers to the award of a lucrative contract to company XYZ Limited by the council's Housing Committee. At the time that the contract was awarded, the press and public were excluded from the committee meeting because of a clause in what's called 'Schedule 12A'. The name of this schedule is unimportant; it is a single schedule at the end of the 1985 Act detailing the type of information which is 'exempt' from public access. In other words, certain categories of information (such as personnel matters, details of individual recipients of council services, legal proceedings and the like) can be conducted in closed session – and so can the award of council contracts. But only up to a certain point.

Clause 9 of Part I of the schedule states that one category of exempt information is 'Any terms proposed by or to the authority in the course of negotiations for a contract for the acquisition or disposal of property or the supply of goods or services'. Which is quite straightforward, and which council officers are willing to quote until you lose interest in seeing the documents. But clause 4 of the Part II schedule of qualifications of those exemptions states: 'Information falling within paragraph 9 of Part I above is exempt information *if and so long as disclosure to the public of the terms would prejudice the authority in those or any other negotiations concerning the property or goods or services* (emphasis added). What this means is that once a contract has been awarded, the disclosure of, say, competitive tendering bids can no longer be prejudicial to the award of that contract to XYZ Limited. Therefore the documents enter the public domain, and are available for public inspection once the contract has been awarded. But local government officers do not give up that easily, so it is useful to follow a few simple guidelines when applying for information from a council:

- Telephone the appropriate council department before visiting their offices to clarify who, exactly, deals with such a request for information. Try to find out the name of the department that maintains a particular register, its location if it is not based at the council's main offices, and the name of the appropriate officer.

- Visit the appropriate department to ask for access to the information that is being sought. If the council refuses to supply that information, keep a diary from that moment detailing all visits, conversations, telephone calls and other communications.

- Following a refusal, put your request in writing to the council's Chief Executive and keep a photocopy of your letter. Give the Chief Executive a week or two to reply. In the meantime, become an expert on the exact piece of law that gives you the right to that information. Find out from the library if it has a copy of the Local Government (Access to Information) Act 1985, and if it has then get to know it in considerable detail. Become an expert on the schedule of exemptions and the further schedule of qualifications.

- Keep up the pressure – and do not take 'No' for an answer. Remember, we live in a democracy and local government has a Freedom of Information Act; local councils are not handling military secrets, they are providing a range of important public services.

- Keep up the diary, and keep the correspondence going until you get access to the information to which you are entitled. If the dispute goes around in circles then involve your local councillor, or another council member with a fighting spirit and a sense of justice. If all else fails go to the local press with your complaint. Keep it simple and sensible, and do not exaggerate the facts – the truth will do. Try to engineer events so that it becomes a dispute between the council and the local community via the local press. Also involve the local Members of Parliament, if they are anything more than back-bench lobby fodder. They can table parliamentary questions and raise the matter very publicly with the appropriate government minister.

• Use a little lateral thinking: if the council is obstructive over the Local Government (Access to Information) Act 1985, then undertake a survey of the council's compliance with the dozens of obscure legal provisions listed in this chapter that requires it to make information available to the public. Conduct a mini-survey of how it performs and then send the results to the local newspapers. And good luck throughout!

Here is the list of those dozens of obscure legal provisions requiring local government authorities to make information available to the press and public:

Local authority accounts. Under the Local Government Finance Act 1982 members of the public have the right to inspect the accounts of a local authority and 'inspect the accounts to be audited and all books, deeds, contracts, bills, vouchers and receipts relating to them and make copies of all or any part of the accounts and those other documents'. This really is an investigation that 'follows the paper trail' in terms of local government activities, and should allow the campaigner or journalist the opportunity to conduct a thorough investigation into an authority's financial affairs. However, this opportunity only occurs once a year, and is usually announced very discreetly with an official notice appearing in the ads columns of a local newspaper (a requirement under the law). So keep your eyes peeled for the advert, although there is nothing to stop a quick call being made to the council's finance department to ask when the next audit is likely to take place. The Accounts and Audit Regulations 1983 (Statutory Instrument 83/1761) then details the way in which the audit has to be conducted. This provides that the accounts and all those other documents are only available for inspection for a two-week period (stated in the advert), and then the opportunity to inspect them is lost forever. The government's Audit Commission, which is the official local government watchdog, has published an excellent guide *Local Government Audit Law* (HMSO) which at around £20 is the authority on the subject. See if your local library can obtain a copy.

'Orders for the payment of money'. Section 228 of the Local Government Act 1972 allows any local government elector for the area of the local authority the right to inspect, and make copies of, an 'order for the payment of money'. The Act does not define the meaning of that term but the public nevertheless has the right to inspect such orders. Try arguing it this way: when a local government spends money, it does not do so because an officer simply gets the urge to spend money – it does so because a decision-making body (i.e. a committee), or an officer with delegated powers, makes a decision to spend money in a particular way. Therefore, 'an order for the payment of money' could be a written record of that decision. It could also refer to an internal requisition from the committee or officer to the finance department to issue a cheque in relation to the proposed transaction. This provision can be a very useful tool for digging around inside a local authority's accounts.

Councillors' expenses. Local authorities are required to 'keep records of all payments to members . . . indicating the amounts paid to each member and the heading under which they were paid'. Paragraph 5(2) of the Local Government (Allowances) (Amendment) (No.2) Regulations 1981 states that electors for the area of the local authority are entitled to inspect those records of the payment of money.

Documents 'deposited with the council'. Specific documents may be required to be deposited with an appointed officer of an authority either by an Act of Parliament, or a Statutory Instrument or in compliance with the Standing Orders of either of the Houses of Parliament. A person interested in such a document may inspect it. This provision is even more obscure than Section 228, but it might be worth investigating on the off chance.

By-laws. These are minor laws that the council has the power to make via the delegated authority of parliament. All by-laws introduced by a local authority must be available for inspection at the offices of that authority, and copies must be available for purchase at a maximum rate of 20 pence each.

Public sewers and drains. Section 32(1) of the Public Health Act 1936 requires councils to keep at their offices a map showing the location of all public sewers and drains within their district. Members of the public may inspect the map at all reasonable hours free of charge.

Education committee minutes. Further to the Local Government (Access to Information) Act 1985, under Paragraph 9 of Part 11 of Schedule 1 of the Education Act 1944, any local government elector has the right to inspect the minutes of proceedings of the education committee on payment of a fee not exceeding 5 pence. And any such person has the right to make a copy of those committee minutes.

Disabled persons' and old persons' homes. Section 37(8) of the National Assistance Act 1948 provides members of the public with the right to inspect the register of disabled persons and old persons homes kept by the county council, and on the payment of a small fee may take copies of the register.

Nurseries and child minding. Section 1(1) of the Nurseries and Childminders Act 1948 provides members of the public with the right to inspect the register kept by the county council containing details of (i) premises, other than premises wholly or mainly used as private dwellings, where children are looked after; and (ii) childminders who are paid to look after children under the age of five.

Commons. Under Section 3(2) of the Commons Registration Act 1965, members of the public have the right to inspect the register maintained by the registering authority (usually the local district or metropolitan authority) containing details of all common land, town and village greens, and the ownership of rights over them.

Young offenders. Section 19(6) of the Children and Young Persons Act 1969, as amended by Section 21 of the Criminal Justice Act 1982, allows members of the public to inspect a copy of any scheme made by the local authority which specifies the arrangements for the treatment of young offenders by the imposition of a supervision order, and the requirements that may be contained in that order. A copy of the scheme must be kept available at the principal office of every authority which is party to the scheme, and a copy provided free of charge to any person requesting one. This would usually be held by the social services department.

Register of planning applications. Section 34(3) of the Town and Country Planning Act 1990 allows members of the public to inspect the statutory planning register relating to planning applications and their results for each address in the authority's area.

Buildings of special interest. Section 54(8) of the Town and Country Planning Act 1990 allows members of the public to see copies of any list supplied by the Secretary of State to a local authority containing details of buildings in the area of special or architectural interest.

Tree preservation orders. Paragraph 4(2) of the schedule to the Town and Country Planning (Tree Preservation Order) Regulations 1969 gives members of the public the right to see, at all reasonable hours, all applications for consent to cut down or lop trees which are subject to a Tree Preservation Order. The public is also entitled to inspect a register of applications for consent work under Tree Preservation Orders and their results at all reasonable hours. Another register that the public is entitled to inspect relates to details of notifications by persons intending to carry out acts affecting trees in conservation areas and the subsequent decision of the district council.

Enforcement actions. The Town and Country Planning Act gives members of the public the right to see at all reasonable hours the register kept by the district planning authority of Enforcement Notices (served where there is a breach of planning control) and Stop Notices (served to prohibit any activity complained of in an enforcement notice) in their area.

Electoral and boundary reviews. Section 60(2)(c) of the Local Government Act 1972 requires a district council or the English or Welsh Local Government Boundary Commission which is proposing to conduct a review relating to the changes in local government areas or electoral arrangements to deposit copies of: (i) draft proposals or recommendations; (ii) any draft order containing changes in electoral arrangements; or (iii) any interim decision not to make any proposals, recommendations or orders; at the offices of a principal council whose areas may be affected. Any such council is required to keep the copies available for inspection at their offices for a period specified by the district council or the appropriate commission.

Section 60(4)(b) of the 1972 Act requires the English or Welsh Boundary Commission which proposes to modify any proposal made by the district council to make changes in local government areas or electoral arrangements, to deposit copies of any draft modification at the offices of any principal council whose area may be affected. Any such council is required to keep the copies available for public inspection at their office for a period specified by the commission.

Section 60(5)(b) requires the English or Welsh Boundary Commission or a district council which makes a report or recommendation in respect of changes in local government areas or electoral arrangements, to deposit copies of the report, proposal or recommendation at the offices of any principal council whose area may be affected. Any such council is required to keep the copies available for public inspection for a period of six months from the date of the order which brings the proposal into effect.

Ombudsman investigations. Section 30(4) of the Local Government Act 1974 provides members of the public with the right to inspect reports of investigations made by the ombudsman (the Local Government Commissioner) undertaken as a result of a written complaint made by, or on behalf of, a person who claims to have suffered injustice as a consequence of maladministration. The right of inspection lasts for three weeks from the date of the report being served on the local authority, and the council is also required to place an advertisement in a newspaper that circulates in the area of that authority giving notice that the investigation has been carried out. However, the Local Government Commissioner may direct that in the interests of the public and the complainant the report is not available for inspection. Generally, past reports of investigations into local authorities are available direct from the Commissioner whose address for further information is 21 Queen Anne's Gate, London, SW1H 9BU. Telephone: 0171–915 3210.

Waste disposal. The Control of Pollution Act 1974 Section 6(4) requires county councils in England, and district councils in Wales, to keep available for public inspection at their main offices at all reasonable hours, a register of all licences issued and currently in force for waste disposal. Copies of entries on the register may be obtained on payment of a reasonable fee.

Noise abatement. Section 64(7) of the Control of Pollution Act 1974 provides members of the public with the right to inspect the noise level register which contains a record of measurement of the level of noise emanating from premises within a noise abatement zone. Copies of entries on the register may be obtained on payment of a reasonable fee, and the register must be available for inspection at the main offices of the council.

Atmospheric pollution. Section 82(5) of the Control of Pollution Act 1974 entitles the public to inspect at all reasonable hours the register of information on atmospheric pollution. Copies of the register may be obtained on payment of a reasonable fee.

Planning inquiries. The Town and Country Planning (Inquiries Procedure) Rules 1974 apply to local inquiries and hearings held in connection with any application or appeal to the Secretary of State in relation to: (i) the Town and Country Planning Act; (ii) Tree Preservation orders; (iii) Listed Building consent orders; and (iv) Control of Advertisement orders. Rule 6(4) provides a right of inspection and copying of the local planning authority's inquiry statement and related documentation by the applicant and any parties who objected to an application. Rule 6(5) allows for any person to inspect and, where practicable, copy the Secretary of State's pre-inquiry statement, the local planning authority's statement and related documentation and any representations submitted by the applicant.

Planning appeals. Under the Town and Country Planning Appeal (Determination by Appointed Persons) (Inquiries Procedure) Rules 1971, Rule 7(3) allows the public the right of inspection and, where practicable, copying of the local planning authority's statement and related documents by the applicant and parties who object to the application. Rule 7(4) provides for any other person to be permitted to inspect and, where practicable, copy the local planning authority's inquiry statement and related documents and any statement submitted by the appellant.

Reservoirs. Section 2(2) of the Resevoirs Act 1975 provides the public with the right to inspect the register maintained by county councils and London boroughs which shows the raised resevoirs in their area, and also provides further information about each such reservoir. The register is available for inspection at the principal office of the authority at all reasonable hours.

Land charges. The Local Land Charges Act 1975, Section 8, allows members of the public to inspect the local land charges register kept by the district council or London borough. The register, which is usually only of interest to solicitors undertaking conveyancing, will show if the specified building is in a conservation area or a smoke control zone; if planning permission has been granted for any purpose; if it is a listed building; if the road has been adopted by the local council; and if there are any footpath rights, tree preservation orders or the like. It does not, however, show the ownership of the building. And the cost of carrying out a search of the register can be high – £20–£25 in some boroughs.

Noise insulation. Noise Insulation Regulations 1975, Regulation 6(3), requires the highway authority to maintain a list of every property which: (i) is eligible for a noise insulation grant, and (ii) has had noise insulation work carried out by the highway authority or its agent. This list or map must be available for public inspection for a period of six months from the date on which the appropriate highway was first open to public traffic.

Highways public inquiries. The Highways (Inquiries Procedure) Rule of 1976 regulate local inquiries into the construction and improvement of trunk special and side roads and associated public works. Rule 10(3) allows the public who are affected by such works, or who have objected to them, to inspect and copy the promoting authority's statement and any supporting documents which it intends to refer to the inquiry. Rule 10(4) provides the right for any person to inspect and, where practicable, copy the promoting authority's statement and supporting documents.

Compulsory purchase orders. The Compulsory Purchase by Public Authorities (Inquiries Procedure) Rules 1976 regulate public inquiries into a local authority's plans to acquire land by means of compulsory purchase. Rule 4(6) allows members of the public who have been served with a notice of the proposed purchase, and who have objected to it, to inspect and, where practicable, to copy: (i) the statement of the authority which proposes the compulsory purchase of the land and (ii) all documents that the authority intends to refer to or present as evidence to the inquiry. Rule 4(7) allows any member of the public to inspect and, where practicable, copy the authority's statement and supporting documents.

Direct labour organizations. The Local Government Planning and Land Act 1980, Section 18(3), allows members of the public the right to inspect the local authority's annual report on construction and maintenance work. A copy of the report may be obtained on the payment of a reasonable fee.

Underused land. Section 96(3) of the Local Government Planning and Land Act 1980 entitles members of the public to inspect at the local authority's principal office, a copy of the register of land holdings. The register contains details of land owned by the local authority which, in the opinion of the Secretary of State, is not being used sufficiently for the performing of the local authority's functions. Section 96(4) allows that a copy of any information contained on the register may be obtained on payment of a reasonable fee. Paragraph 3(5) of Schedule 32 allows any person to inspect the copy of an enterprise zone planning scheme kept at the principal office of a local authority. Copies may be obtained free of charge.

Highways. Section 36(7) of the Highways Act 1980 requires all county councils and London boroughs to prepare a list of streets in their area which are highways maintainable at the public expense. Such a list may be inspected free of charge and at all reasonable hours at the offices of the council concerned, and also at the offices of all district councils within the county. Section 37(5) gives members of the public the right to inspect free of charge and at all reasonable hours: (i) certificates of acceptance of private highways 'dedicated' to a local authority; and (ii) orders made by the local magistrates' court transferring responsibility for the maintenance of highways to the local authority so that they are maintained at the public expense.

Wildlife and Countryside Act 1981. Section 57(5) requires the county council and London boroughs to keep definitive maps and statements showing public rights of way along footpaths, bridleways and public paths. These maps are open to public inspection free of charge and at all reasonable hours. They should be available for public inspection in the borough to which they refer. Paragraph 3(8) (a) of Schedule 15 allows members of the public to inspect and take copies of any document which the local authority took into account in the preparation of the definitive map.

Education. Regulation 5(4) of the Education (School Information) Regulations 1981 requires that information relating to schools admissions arrangements must be published and made available for public inspection. Regulation 6(4) provides details on how information relating to special schools should be published.

Planning Enforcement Notice and Appeals. The Town and Country Planning (Enforcement) (Inquiries Procedure) Rules 1981 makes a number of provisions for access to information. An appellant has the right to inspect and copy the documents that the local planning authority intends to refer to or to present as evidence, at the inquiry. Any other person has the right to inspect and copy the local planning authority's statement about a government department's or local authority's views, and inquiry documents and any representations served by the appellant. And any other person has the right to inspect and copy the local planning authority's pre-inquiry statement.

Generating Stations and Overhead Lines. The Electricity Stations and Overhead Lines (Inquiries Procedures) Rules 1981 govern inquiries into applications by electricity suppliers for consent to construct or extend a generating station on any land or for consent to place an overhead electric line other than a consumer line or a line within premises owned by the electricity supplier. The applicant and objectors to the application have the right to inspect and copy the local planning authority's pre-inquiry statement and supporting documents.

Rent and rate rebates. The Social Security and Housing Benefits Act 1982, Section 31(i) (b) and (c), requires local authorities granting rent rebates and rent allowances under a statutory or local scheme to: (i) make available for public inspection at their principal office and at all reasonable hours and free of charge, copies of the scheme; and (ii) in the case of a local scheme, provide a copy to any person on payment of a reasonable fee.

Structure and local plans. The Town and Country Planning (Structure and Local Plans) Regulations 1982 govern the preparation and public inspection of the structure and local plans. These are major plans for the future development of towns and cities known as

Development Plans. Regulation 37 states that the public has the right to inspect at all reasonable hours copies of the structure and local plans at the council's main office 'and at such other places as the authority deems appropriate' and without fee. A statement setting out the rights to question the validity of the plans must also be available for inspection. Separate regulations apply the same rights for boroughs in the Greater London area.

Elections. The Representation of the People Act 1983 under Section 89(1) allows the public to see all returns and declarations and accompanying documents sent by a candidate of a parliamentary or council election to the appropriate returning officer relating to election expenses. This right lasts for a period of two years from the date that the documents are received by the council, and a small fee can be charged for inspection and photocopies.

Workforce statistics. The Local Government (Publication of Manpower Information) (England) Regulations require local authorities to publish quarterly statements each year showing the number of their full-time and part-time manual and non-manual employees overall, and in relation to the different service categories. The statements must also show any change in these numbers since the preceding quarter and also comparisons with other authorities. Similar regulations also apply in Wales.

Residential care. Section 7 of the Registered Homes Act 1984 provides the public with the right to inspect a register maintained by the council's social services department of care homes and the persons in control of such homes. The register can be inspected at all reasonable times and upon the payment of a reasonable fee.

Advertisements. The Town and Country Planning (Control of Advertisements) Regulations 1984, under Regulation 31(5), allows the public to inspect a register kept by the local planning authority for consent applications to display advertisements (such as the large advertising hoardings) on land, and the decision of the authority.

Housing. The Housing Act 1985 allows a number of rights of access to local authority housing information. They are:

Section 105(5): This requires a published arrangement for housing management (i) to be available for public inspection at the landlord authority's principal office at all reasonable hours and without charge; and (ii) to be provided to any member of the public on payment of a reasonable fee. A landlord authority is a local authority (usually the district or borough council) which provides housing accommodation and related facilities.

Section 105(6): This requires a landlord authority which is a registered housing association to send a copy of the published arrangements for housing management to (i) the Housing Corporation and (ii) the district council or London borough in which the housing association lets properties under secured tenancies.

Section 106(2): The public has the right to inspect documents that set out the rules of a landlord authority for determining priority between applicants for housing, and the rules for the transfer of tenants. These can be inspected at all reasonable hours at the authority's principal office.

Section 106(3): A copy of the rules should be available at the offices of the district council or London borough in which there are dwelling houses let under secure tenancies. These can be inspected free of charge at all reasonable hours.

Section 106(4): This permits members of the public to request a copy of (i) the summary of published information on housing allocation, for which there is no fee; and (ii) a copy of the rules referred to in the section above, for which a reasonable fee can be charged.

Section 106(5): Applicants to a local authority for housing are entitled to a copy of the details that they have supplied to the housing authority about themselves in their application for accommodation. This information is available at all reasonable times and without charge.

Section 349: Members of the public have the right to see at all reasonable hours a copy of the registration scheme kept by the local housing authority containing details of houses in multiple occupation and those with poor sanitary conditions. A copy can be obtained on request for a small fee.

Section 414(3): Members of the public are entitled to inspect the register kept by the local housing authority of common lodging houses, which are houses other than public assistance institutions, provided to accommodate poor persons for the purposes of sleeping and eating. This register can be inspected without fee, and certified copies of an entry in the register are available from the authority.

Land Registry Act 1988

Until 1988 the details of the owners of some 13 million properties and plots of land registered on Her Majesty's Land Registry (an organization almost as secretive as the security services) were kept strictly confidential, and the only person able to access these records were the landowners themselves or their nominated representatives, such as solicitors or accountants. In the words of a spokesperson for the Country Landowners Association, which represents some 49,000 landholders who own 80 per cent of agricultural land in Britain, 'land ownership is a private matter and not something for every busybody in the country to get their hands on'. An Englishman's home, it seemed, was truly his castle. But the Land Registration Act 1988 put an end to all that.

The thinking behind the Act was that businesses and individuals might, say, need the information on the ownership of neighbouring properties before applying for planning permission. However, the Land Registry records clearly demonstrate that there is a difference between openness and accessibility of information. The Act provides a convoluted route that has to be followed before the necessary information can be obtained. To start with, the Land Registry holds details only of *registered* land, and not all land or property. If a piece of land or property has changed hands at any time since 1925, when routine land registration began, the ownership details will be recorded at the appropriate Land Registry office. However, some 9 million properties of the approximately 22 million properties in England and Wales are not registered in this way, and ownership details do not appear on the registry. This particularly includes a large number of properties owned by the Crown, the Church of England, the government and many inherited estates, such as those owned by aristocratic families.

If the land or property in question is registered, the investigator will need to follow a bureaucratic route to obtain details of ownership. To start with, the enquirer will need to know the title number of the property, as the address alone is not sufficient: the registry files are organized on the basis of the chronological title numbers. To find the title number, the enquirer will have to undertake a search of the Registry's Public Index Map which details every piece of registered land. The Public Index Map will also detail whether a piece of registered land is freehold or leasehold, and an inspection fee of £5 is charged for this service. The search can be done by post on Land Registry Form 96.

Once the title number is known, the register itself can be inspected, and there are three separate and distinct parts to the register. The first part is the Property Register, which identifies the geographical location and extent of the registered property, usually by detailing the postal address and also by reference to a large-scale Ordnance Survey map. This entry will detail any public rights of way on or near the property, or other legal rights that may affect the use of, or access to, the property.

The second part of the Register is the Proprietorship Register, which will be of particular use to an investigative enquiry as it reveals the owner of the property. This entry on the register also details any legal restrictions on the owner's right to sell the property, should there be any type of mortgage or loan secured against it.

The third part of the register is the Charges Register which contains details of any such registered mortgages or other financial matters registered on that particular property. These registered entries are all obtainable by post by using Land Registry Form 109 together with a further fee of £5. Copies of these forms, an explanatory leaflet and a list of the appropriate charges in force are available from any of the 18 Land Registry district offices around the country, which are listed in the telephone directory. Alternatively, the forms are available from the head office of Her Majesty's Land Registry, Lincoln's Inn Fields, London, WC2A 3PH. Tel: 0171–917 8888.

During the early 1990s, the Land Registry started a multi-million pound computerization process to ease the process of conducting searches on property ownership. One of these services is to feed in a proprietor's name and print out a list of the registered properties registered as being owned by that individual – a service that is available for a £10 fee. The problem with this system, however, is that a property might be registered as being owned by a company or individual nominee, and not by the actual owner under investigation. Undertaking a search of individual proprietors can be a hit-or-miss business that ends up costing a small fortune. In Northern Ireland, however, the system is already fully computerized and provides a taste of things to come elsewhere in the United Kingdom. The Northern Ireland Land Registry has a combined computer system comprising digitized Ordnance Survey maps of the entire region cross-referenced to the computerized records of individual property ownership.

Another way that property ownership details can be searched, particularly if there is no registered title at the Land Registry, is by simply making discreet enquiries with neighbours and, failing that, the local reference library press cuttings files. And bear in mind that the local authority Statutory Planning Register may throw some light on the ownership of the property if an application for planning permission has ever been made for that particular address.

Environmental Protection Act 1990

The public now has considerable new, and almost unheralded, rights to information on pollution through the Environment Protection Act 1990, although these provisions are confused by secrecy clauses remaining in other Acts of Parliament dealing with the environment and pollution-related matters. The Environmental Protection Act 1990 establishes public registers about the most polluting industries, and generally requires the disclosure of applications by companies and others for authorizations to release pollution into the atmosphere; actual authorizations by such bodies as local authorities; pollution monitoring results of environmental surveys conducted by the likes of Her Majesty's Inspectorate of Pollution, the Health and Safety Executive and local authority environmental protection departments; and enforcement actions taken by such agencies. But information can be withheld on the grounds of 'commercial confidentiality' or national security.

Originally, the proposals for public registers were limited to two main areas of pollution: the new system of 'integrated pollution control', which applies to the most severe polluting processes, and waste disposal. Some limited disclosure about radioactive substances was proposed when the Bill was introduced in parliament, but the Bill changed shape considerably as the government accepted additional disclosure provisions during the Bill's passage through parliament. As a result of these amendments, public registers on the hazards of genetically modified organisms and chemically contaminated land have been established, although the government had resisted pressure for statutory registers in these areas. Further disclosure of chemical dumping at sea and litter has also been added.

A number of amendments proposed by environmental campaigners during the passage of the Bill also led to a number of changes to the Bill during its passage through parliament. The Labour MP Ann Taylor persuaded the government not to allow 'commercially confidential' information to be permanently excluded from the public registers. Initially such information would be exempted indefinitely, although the provisions for confidentiality will now lapse after four years unless they are specifically renewed. The Liberal-Democrat peer Lord Tordoff successfully pressed for two further amendments: first, for additional disclosure of chemical dumping and incineration at sea, and then for a clause requiring the public dislosure of the conviction record of any person under the Radioactive Substances Act 1960.

Local authorities were given powers to act against hazardous air pollution under 'statutory nuisance' procedures, which make it a criminal offence for an official to release information about 'any manufacturing process or trade secret' unless the disclosure 'is in the performance of his duty' – and there is no legal duty to keep the public informed. An amendment tabled by Lord Tordoff deleted the reference to 'manufacturing process' so the measure now applies only to actual trade secrets. A further amendment proposed by Lord McIntosh of Haringey requiring the Pollution Inspectorate to disclose reports of their investigations into environmental pollution was rejected by the government, but it resulted in a government undertaking that such reports would be included in the public registers if they related to a 'regulated process'.

The final amendment concerned information about chemical waste withheld because of 'commercial confidentiality'. If such information were withheld a note to that effect had to be placed on the public register. However, the government resisted other amendments proposing that public registers be set up relating to statutory nuisances.

Although a number of amendments were successfully proposed to the Environmental Protection Act 1990, its actual introduction was far from smooth. One reason for this was that although the Act sets down the basic terms for such registers, the precise mechanisms for their operation were detailed in a statutory regulation – the Environmental Protection (Applications, Appeals and Registers) Regulations 1991 – which gave government ministers considerable power to determine the way in which the law would work in practice.

These regulations, however, omitted one major consideration. The authorities would not have to disclose the results of their investigations into the health and environmental implications of pollution or pollution-generating practices. Thus, if a process were established as being life-threatening, this information would not have to be disclosed under the regulations. Intense lobbying by environmental campaigners and freedom of information groups resulted in the appropriate government minister making the following statement in the House of Lords on 8 October 1990: 'I can assure your Lordships that a report on an investigation into pollution of the environment will be made publicly available.' She added that as long as such a report related to a specific process, then 'that . . . should go on the register along with other information about the process. When the draft regulations appeared, this undertaking was left out. The Campaign for Freedom of Information wrote to the Department of the Environment (DOE) reminding it of the minister's statement to the House of Lords, but when the Department amended the draft regulations, it included a clause that required the registers to show 'particulars of any report *published* by an enforcing authority relating to an assessment of the environmental consequences' of a regulated process. If an enforcing authority such as the local council chooses not to formally publish a report, that report need not be included on the public register.

Another weakness in the regulations relates to pollution-monitoring results. Such data would allow the public to see if an industrialist's pollution discharges are within the legal limits, but there are no time limits for such data to be included in the public registers. Therefore if an authority finds that its standards are being flouted, then it can sit on the results for as long as it likes. It could, for example, decide only to update the pollution registers once a year, thus denying the public access to all current information.

These examples of the various problems and difficulties associated with the introduction of what is otherwise a progressive piece of environmental protection law, give an idea of the obstructive tactics that can be used by officials wanting to prevent the implementation of unwelcome legislation. So an investigator wanting to research pollution-related matters should be aware of the various pitfalls. Like other investigations of local government, environmental campaigners could well benefit by recruiting the support of a councillor and local Member of Parliament, who should have access to more detailed information than the general public.

In short, public registers will contain the following information: control of radioactive substances (including radioactive waste); enforcement notices having environmental and public safety implications; industrial processes which could cause 'significant pollution' to air, land and water; licensed dumping at sea; litter control; sites of special scientific interest; genetically modified organisms; stray dogs; waste management licences; carriers of controlled waste, and water pollution and supply. Registers of environmental information are held by Her Majesty's Inspectorate of Pollution, the National Rivers Authority (in Scotland, Her Majesty's Industrial Pollution Inspection and River Purification Authorities), some government departments such as the Health and Safety Executive, local government authorities and water companies. Not all registers are held by each organization, and it is useful to start with the appropriate local council to see what information it holds. Particularly knowledgeable sources of information on such matters should be the local branches of environmental pressure groups such as Friends of the Earth and Greenpeace. Friends of the Earth can be contacted at its head office at 26 Underwood Street, London, N1 7JQ. Telephone 0171- 490 1555. Greenpeace is at Canonbury Villas, London, N1 2HB. Telephone 0171-354 5100. The Department of the Environment publishes an explanatory leaflet entitled *Access to Environmental Information – Your Rights Explained*, which is available from public libraries or direct from the Department of the Environment, Room A132, Romney House, 43 Marsham Street, London, SW1P 3PY; or in Scotland from the Scottish Office Environment Department, Room 269, 27 Perth Street, Edinburgh, EH3 5RB.

Chapter seven

Health Services

THE National Health Service has an annual budget that exceeds £20 billion and is the country's largest employer, with more than a million staff. But it is also a massive bureaucracy that lacks an effective level of public accountability. The NHS therefore provides an ideal study of the way in which an obsessive level of secrecy can apply to an organization that ostensibly is not secretive and has no secrets to keep.

Although local government authorities are required to conduct their business largely in the public gaze because of the Local Government (Access to Information) Act 1985, the National Health Service is not required to comply with these particular 'open door' provisions. Instead, the NHS is regulated by the Public Bodies (Admission to Meetings) Act 1960 – the UK's first ever freedom of information act introduced by a young Conservative back-bench Member of Parliament called Margaret Thatcher (see p.64).

The 1960 Act contains three key requirements. First, the full meetings of regional health authorities and district health authorities must be open to the public. Secondly, a notice advertising the date, time and place of the meeting must be posted at the offices of the health authority for at least three clear days before the meeting. And, thirdly, the press – but not the general public – must on request be supplied with a copy of the agenda ' ... and such further particulars necessary to indicate the nature of any item'.

But a health authority 'may, by way of resolution, exclude the public whenever publicity would be prejudicial to the public interest by reason of the confidential nature of the business to be transacted or for other special reasons ... ' What, though, might that mean, and how might health authorities translate terms such as 'special reasons' in their areas? In 1992 the now-defunct Community Rights Project undertook a questionnaire survey of each regional health authority and district health authority in England and Wales. Each was asked to answer in their own words a number of questions about their compliance (or lack of compliance) with the Public Bodies (Admission to Meetings) Act 1960. Here is a summary of its findings.

Notice of meetings. As we have seen, the law requires health authorities to display a notice giving details of their full meetings. However, the following authorities stated that they did *not* publish such a notice: Bradford, City and Hackney, Gwynedd, Isle of Wight, Lewisham and North Southwark, Mid Glamorgan, Mid Staffordshire, and North West Hertfordshire. Therefore these authorities were, by their own admission, breaking the law. A number of other health authorities were also breaking the law by not posting a notice, but informed the public by other means, such as placing an advertisement in the local newspaper. They were: Bristol and Weston, Central Nottinghamshire, Dartford and Gravesham, Greenwich, Islington, North Hertfordshire, Norwich, Portsmouth, South Bedfordshire, South Birmingham, Southmead, the South West Thames Regional Health Authority, and Waltham Forest. Authorities that went beyond the legal minimum by posting extra notices to encourage the public to attend their meetings were: Basingstoke and North Hampshire, East Birmingham, East Suffolk, Halton, Hampstead, Hillingdon, Kettering, Mid-Downs, Parkside, South Cumbria, South East Kent, South West Surrey, Walsall, and West Lancashire.

Exclusion of the public. Before passing a resolution under the 1960 Act to exclude the press and public from a health authority meeting, the authority must by law consider (i) whether publicity would be prejudicial to the public interest, *and* (ii) the confidential nature of the business to be transacted. The Community Rights Project asked health authorities if they considered *both* (i) and (ii) before passing a resolution to exclude the press and public. The following authorities freely admitted that they did not consider both (i) and (ii) and were therefore breaking the law: Barnsley, Bexley,

NHS Organizational chart

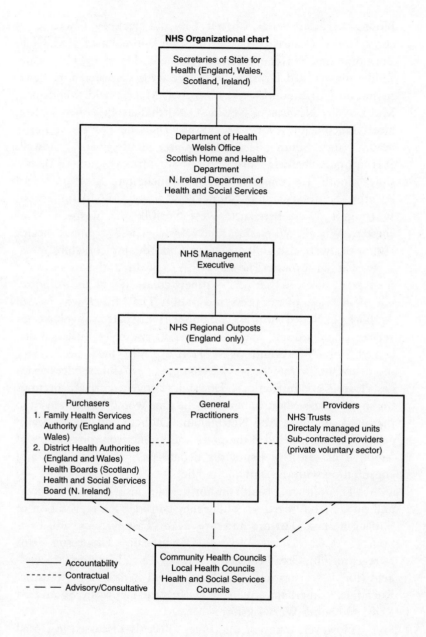

Bloomsbury, Cambridge, Chester, City and Hackney, Clwyd, Coventry, Crewe, Doncaster, Dudley, East Berkshire, East Dyfed, Great Yarmouth and Waveney, Gwent, Gwynedd, Haringey, Harrogate, Kidderminster and District, Leeds Western, Leicestershire, Lewisham and North Southwark, Liverpool, Macclesfield, Maidstone, Mid-Downs, Newcastle, Newham, Northallerton, North Devon, North Lincolnshire, North Tees, North Tyneside, Pontefract, Portsmouth and South East Hampshire, Redbridge, Sandwell, Scarborough, Sheffield, Shropshire, Southampton, Southern Derbyshire, South Lincolnshire, South Manchester, Southport and Formby, South Tyneside, South West Surrey, Waltham Forest, Warrington, West Berkshire, West Norfolk and Wisbech, Winchester, Wirral, Worcester, and York. Three regional health authorities were also guilty: Mersey, Oxford, and Yorkshire.

Closed sessions. The survey asked health authorities to state the type of business that was routinely conducted by the authority out of the view of the press and public. The Mid-Downs Health Authority excluded the press and public from 'matters that have not yet been finalised and therefore may give rise to confusion if discussed publicly'. South West Hertfordshire held preliminary discussions in private 'on service changes or possible services changes, closures and restrictions'. Dewsbury convened private meetings on 'major issues where publicity at the time would be prejudicial to the public interest'. And Nottingham, Oldham and Wigan health authorities also excluded the press and public from discussions of 'emotive or sensitive issues for debate prior to discussion and consultation with the staff and public'.

The following health authorities curiously exclude the press and public from meetings where they consider the registration of nursing homes: Dartford and Graveham, East Birmingham, Eastbourne, East Dyfed, Exeter, Gateshead, Gloucester (for re-registration), Great Yarmouth and Waveney, Islington, Macclesfield (for de-registration), Newham, North Bedfordshire, Preston, Rochdale, Rotherham, Rugby, St Helen's and Knowsley, South East Kent, and South Warwickshire.

However, many of the topics allegedly discussed in closed session were so broad that they could cover most if not all health authority business. Cornwall and the Isles of Scilly discussed in private 'matters which might cause unnecessary alarm to patients and relatives'. North Birmingham excluded the press and public from discussions on 'policy issues' and Norwich did the same in relation to 'private authority matters'. South Bedfordshire debated in private all 'management changes, reports of special interest groups, items of large cost implications, or discussion on major changes to client care prior to discussion in public session ... '; Southport and Formby, 'early warning of potential problems'; Torbay, 'matters of policy, personnel and planning'; and Wirral, 'items of a sensitive nature'. South Sefton stated that its private sessions considered: 'chairmen's reports, problems about the provision of services, membership issues, advisory service reports, and Health Service Commission reports'.

A number of authorities mentioned reports of members' visits to hospitals as examples of business conducted behind closed doors. The Department of Health regards such visits as having a crucial role in monitoring the quality of service provided for patients by the district health authorities. The reports of such visits should, therefore, be in the public domain. But the following health authorities resolved not to discuss such reports in public: Aylesbury Vale, Dudley, Hull, Lancaster, North Birmingham, Southend, and South West Durham. And for some authorities, secrecy seems to have become a mania. Coventry health authority denied the press and public access to 'minutes of previous meetings'. South Derbyshire excluded them from discussion of 'arrangements for members' informal activities'; and Haringey went into secret session to consider 'untouched incidents'.

Public access to committee minutes. Unlike local government authorities, whose minutes of committee and sub-committee meetings must automatically be available for public inspection, the minutes of health authorities can be concealed from the public. The following health authorities engaged in good practice by making available for public inspection all minutes of their committees and sub-committees: Brighton, Camberwell, Central Manchester, Chester, Clywd, Dewsbury, Durham, Ealing, East Cumbria, Great Yarmouth, Gwent, Gwynedd, Haringey, Isle of Wight, Lancaster, Leeds Western, Lewisham and Southwark, Liverpool, North Devon,

North Manchester, Oxfordshire, Pembrokeshire, Portsmouth, Preston, Rotherham, Southampton, South Cumbria, Southport, Stockport, Tameside, Torbay, West Lancashire, West Norfolk and Wisbech, Wolverhampton, North East Thames Regional Health Authority, and Wessex Regional Health Authority.

Under the Public Bodies (Admission to Meetings) Act 1960, health authorities are permitted to set up committees which, in turn, can set up sub-committees. This hierarchy of delegation is specifically and unambiguously stated in a statutory regulation and is thus law. Nevertheless, 52 health authorities indicated that they had sub-committees without any parent committee (with the number of sub-committees in brackets): Blackpool (2+), Bradford (5), Bromley (4), Brighton (4), Bury (2), Central Manchester (2), Central Nottingham (3), Chichester (4), Cornwall (2), Crewe (1), Darlington (4), Dewsbury (4), Dudley (3), East Birmingham (5), East Yorkshire (2+), Gateshead (4), Gwent (1), Hampstead (6), Haringey (7), Hartlepool (3), Herefordshire (7), Islington (11), Kidderminster (3), Kingston and Esher (4+), Leicestershire (1), Macclesfield (5), Maidstone (3), Mid Staffordshire (4), Newham (3), Northallerton (3), North Derbyshire (2), North Devon (3), North East Essex (3), North Hertfordshire (2), North Tees (3), North Tyneside (8), Redbridge (8), St Helens (7), Knowsley (4), Salford (3), Shropshire (1), South Glamorgan (6), South Manchester (4), South West Durham (6), Tameside and Glossop (3), Wakefield (4), Walsall (8), Warrington (1), West Birmingham (1), Winchester (4), Wolverhampton (as required), York (1).

Twenty health authorities said they had no committees. In itself this does not necessarily mean that these authorities are less secretive than any others. Yet it is possible within those authorities to find contradictory attitudes to secrecy and public access to information. On the positive side, Peterborough District Health Authority stated that if it ever had any committees or sub-committees they would be open to the public. However, South Tyneside District Health Authority emphasized that if it were ever to set up committees, it would certainly exclude the public, and added: 'If we had closed sub-committees we would obtain members views without running the risk of advance publicity.'

The worst culprits. The survey reveals that the following district health authorities neither allow their members to attend committee meetings of which they are not a member, nor provide full minutes of committee meetings to the members of the full authority: Bexley, Cornwall, East Hertfordshire (under review), Enfield, Harrow, North Birmingham, Redbridge, Riverside, Scarborough, Somerset, South Bedfordshire, South Lincolnshire, South Tees, Wakefield (under review), Wirral, and Yorkshire Regional Health Authority. The following health authorities did not reply to the survey: Bassetlaw, Croydon, Hastings, Huddersfield, Huntingdon, Mid Surrey, North West Surrey, Plymouth, Powys, Swindon, West Cumbria, West Surrey and North East Hampshire, South Western Regional Health Authority and the Trent Regional Health Authority. And Bromsgrove and Redditch District Health Authority declined to complete the questionnaire unless they received a payment from the Community Rights Project. The District General Manager wrote: 'Health authorities are currently being inundated with requests for information' and that the fee for completing the questionnaire would depend upon 'how time consuming it is to provide this information'. So much for accountability. However, the Community Rights Project later asked the Bromsgrove and Redditch Health Authority for copies of the minutes of its main authority meetings, which they supplied free of charge.

The first conclusion from this research is that this type of data provides local journalists and community campaigners with enough leads to launch their own investigations into the operation and internal management of their local district health authorities. But it also confirms that having a law such as the Public Bodies (Admission to Meetings) Act 1960 – or even the Local Government (Access to Information) Act 1985 in many cases – is not enough. A combination of the political will to make such laws work, and the administrative mechanisms to enforce this type of access-to-information law, are also needed. The other factor about regional and district health authorities is that their members are not democratically elected representatives accountable to the electorate at the ballot box every three or four years. They are appointed by the Secretary of State at the Department of Health, and are often appointed for being good Establishment men (or, occasionally, women) who will not rock the boat or upset the status quo by demanding changes to the decision-making processes. Indeed, the background of such appointees – the political allegiances and business interests of health authority members – could also be a fruitful area of investigation for the journalist or campaigner who wants to uncover the way in which power is allocated at a local level, and to establish if such appointments are a form of regional or local political decoration.

The Hospitals and Health Services Year Book. This is a huge directory to all aspects of the National Health Service and independent medical sector that is published each year by the Institute of Health Services Management and may be regarded as the Bible on the NHS. It contains a range of directories of regional and district health authorities, NHS Trusts, general practice fund holders, family health services authorities, the Northern Ireland Health and Personal Social Services Boards, London postgraduate teaching hospitals, Ministry of Defence hospitals, and special and state hospitals (such as Broadmoor). Each of these entries contains detailed background information on each authority, such as the number and types of hospitals and clinics, and the identity of key personnel and board or authority members. This directory also has sections on the independent health sector, local authorities, government departments and agencies, statutory bodies, health service finance, statutory instruments and circulars, negotiating bodies for the health service, and various indexes.

As an example of the type of information that a directory of this nature can produce, take a look at the section entitled 'Statutory Instruments and Circulars' (bearing in mind, of course, just how dull investigative research can be – according to the various experts quoted in the introduction to this book.) In the almost endless list of statutory instruments and orders is one entitled *The NHS (Audit of Accounts of Health Authorities) Regulations 1982* which is described as '... making provisions relating to the audit of accounts of all regional and district health authorities, all special trustees of certain university or teaching hospitals and the Dental Estimates Board *and in particular for the production of documents and information ...*' (emphasis added).

In the event of a dispute over information on the accounts of a health authority, this regulation would be well worth investigating in a law library or with the local community health council.

Community Health Council. Bearing in mind the size and complexity of the National Health Service – and the obvious disadvantage its users are normally at if there is a problem or if they have a complaint – in 1974 the government set up and funded a network of Community Health Councils (CHCs) to act as local watchdogs and represent the public in the event of a dispute or disagreement over the provision of local health services. Some CHCs are dynamic research and campaigning bodies that exert considerable influence within the district health authority; others merely pay lip-service to the local NHS management, and otherwise keep a low public profile. There are 211 CHCs in England and Wales who keep under review the operation of the health services in their districts and recommend improvements. They have to be consulted on any substantial development or variation in services. CHCs were set up in response to evidence that NHS care was not sufficiently patient-centred and to make a clear distinction between the management and public representation functions of the National Health Service. CHCs were given the role of representing the local community to the management of the local health service. The budgets and staffing of CHCs are the responsibility of the regional health authorities, and of the Welsh Office in Wales, and there are variations in both throughout England and Wales. CHCs have been involved in the process of opening up the NHS to the public, and anyone intending to undertake detailed research into a local district health authority or NHS trust can do little better than call in on the local Community Health Council: they are listed in the telephone directory under 'Community Health Councils'. Normally, the local CHC will be in receipt of all agendas, minutes, accounts, annual reports and many background documents and reports. The secretary of the CHC should be able to explain the decision-making process of the local health authority and trust, and should be able to provide background information on the members and officers of the health authority management.

The Community Health Council itself is subject to an access-to-information law, the Commununity Health Councils (Access to

Information) Act 1988 which parallels the Local Government (Access to Information) Act 1985. This means that meetings of its committees and sub-committees must be open to the public, as must their minutes and background reports. Section 2(1) of the Community Health Councils (Access to Information) Act 1988 states: 'A Community Health Council shall maintain a register containing the name and address of every member of the Council and of every committee appointed by the Council whether alone or jointly with another Council and stating in the case of each member of the Council – (a) the name and address of the body which appointed him; (b) whether or not he is a member of that body; (c) in the case of a member appointed by a voluntary organisation (within the meaning of the National Health Service Act 1977), that he has been so appointed.'

Section 2(2) states: 'A written summary of the rights – (a) to attend meetings of a Community Health Council and community health committee, and (b) to inspect and copy, and be furnished with documents relating to such a Council or committee, which are for the time being conferred by virtue of section 1 above shall be kept at the offices of each such council.'

The Act goes on to say in Section 2(3): 'The register maintained by a Council under subsection (1) above and the summary kept by it under subsection (2) above shall be open to inspection by the public at all reasonable hours and without payment at the offices of the Council; and any person may, on payment of such reasonable fee as the Council may determine – (a) make copies of or of extracts from any such register or summary kept by it; and (b) require the Council to supply him before the end of the period of three days beginning with the day on which the request is made with a photographic copy of or of extracts from any such register or summary.'

In its annual report for 1992/93, the Association of Community Health Councils for England and Wales (ACHCEW), which represents the majority of the 211 community Health Councils, referred to a number of issues concerning public access to health authority meetings and information. On the subject of NHS Trusts, it warned that trust boards are only required to meet in public once a year, and are not required to consult about major changes in their services. Some 40 per cent of CHCs reported that their local boards held formal meeting around 10–12 times a year; 36 per cent stated that their local boards met formally only 4–6 times a year; and 18 per cent met formally only 1–3 times a year. Fifty per cent of CHCs are never invited to formal trust board meetings, although 46 per cent are always invited. Fifty-one per cent stated that they were never sent any of the background papers on the business of the meetings although 38 per cent were always supplied with the documentation.

The secretary of one Community Health Council is quoted as saying: 'We are given, informally, information about changes – usually by Medical Directors or business managers – often in confidence. We meet, informally, with the Chief Executive and Chairman bi-monthly. We are told of all the good things that they are doing. We are not told of the extent of their financial difficulties or the cuts made to stay within budget. We get this information through other sources such as staff who moan to members during CHC visits.'

On the subject of district health authorities, the ACHCEW report states that only one quarter of District Health Authorities hold formal meetings 10–12 times a year. Before the NHS reforms it was commonplace for all health authorities to meet that frequently. Now some 62 per cent of district health authorities meet only 4–6 times a year. This means that many decisions are made by the authority 'informally' outside of these meetings and away from public scrutiny. The report goes on to say that all Community Health Councils, except for one (unspecified), are invited to all formal meetings of the District Health Authority. Ninety-seven per cent are given speaking rights at the meetings, and 90 per cent are provided with background papers. The National Association of Community Health Councils for England and Wales is at 30 Drayton Park, London, N5 1PB. Telephone: 0171-609 8405.

Family Health Services Authority. The Family Health Services Authority is the local body responsible for managing the NHS services provided away from hospitals and clinics by general practitioners, dentists, pharmacists and ophthalmic practitioners. The routine promotional material sent out by FHSAs usually describes their service along the following lines: 'The Family Health Services Authority exists to ensure that the communities it serves get the best possible care from local general practices. A full list of all practices is published each year by the FHSA and contains information about the services offered by each of them, the languages spoken by staff at the practice and other details. All general practices, dentists, pharmacists and opticians have a copy of this local directory, as do libraries, local health authority offices, Community Health Councils, health clinics, and advice centres. The Directory also gives details of all dentists, community pharmacists and opthalmic practitioners in the area.' The Family Health Services Authority is a separate organization altogether from the District Health Authority or NHS trust, and is also scrutinized by the network of local Community Health Councils. The same ACHCEW annual report has this to say about family health services authorities: 'Sadly, relations between CHCs and FHSAs have deteriorated sharply since the [NHS] reforms. While the number of CHCs reporting poor or very poor relations remains low (five per cent), very good relations now make up just 18 per cent of the total, compared to 45 per cent before the reforms.' The report then goes on to warn that: 'CHCs call their FHSAs "stuffy", "secretive and defensive", "useless and powerless". But one CHC boasts of a "very open relationship – CHC recognised as constructive in helping plan and develop services".' So the local Family and Health Services Authority might well be another powerhouse worthy of the attentions of the investigative researcher or journalist.

Joint local authority/health authority bodies. The local government authority and local health authority are separate and distinct bodies. The council is regulated by the Local Government (Access to Information) Act 1985 and, as we have seen, the health authority is regulated by the Public Bodies (Admission to Meetings) Act 1960. But sometimes the two get together and form joint committees for a specific purpose. This is usually to deal with a public health issue where the two organizations have an interest in the subject: port health authorities are an example. In such a case another act of parliament – the Health Service Joint Committee (Access to Information) Act 1986 – swings into action. This generally provides the same rights as the Local Government (Access to Information) Act 1985, viz: meetings must be announced and publicized in advance; the public must be allowed to attend such meetings; copies of agenda, minutes and background reports and documents must be available for public inspection and copying.

Specialist organizations. Branches of various specialist organizations, charities and pressure groups with an interest in health matters will normally exist within the area of each health authority. These might include carers associations, local groups of the National Association of Mental Health (MIND), MENCAP, or branches of the health service unions such as Unison or the Royal College of Nursing. Their activities and effectiveness will vary from area to area and have as much to do with the individual personalities of local officers as with other resources. But particularly active groups will probably have a thorough working knowledge of the local health services, and could be an invaluable source of local intelligence. The local reference library will normally have a directory or file on such groups.

The College of Health. One particularly resourceful self-help health campaigning group that operates at a national level is the College of Health. The College has six main declared areas of activity: to help people keep themselves healthy; to help people look after themselves better when they are ill; to give people the information they need to make the most effective use of the NHS; to improve the quality of communication between doctors and their patients; to campaign for a better deal for health service consumers; and to inform people about sources of help outside the NHS, for example from self-help groups and voluntary organizations for people who suffer from particular diseases, disabilities and handicaps. Part of that process is served by a computerized register operated by the College that details over 1,200 self-help groups and organizations throughout the country. The College of Health is at: 21 Old Ford Road, London, E2 9PL. Telephone 0181-983 1225.

Companies. Given the growth of the private medical sector, it should not be overlooked that some health organizations will be limited companies and be required to furnish a mass of information as described in Chapter 5. This may apply to private clinics, nursing homes and hospitals, and even the local NHS Trust may be registered as a 'company limited by guarantee' – a non-profit-making company that benefits from limited liability status. A good way of checking if an organization is a limited company is to scrutinize its headed notepaper or visit the main office to look for a notice displaying the company details.

Ombudsman. The NHS Ombudsman, or Health Service Commissioner, is empowered to investigate a variety of problems in the NHS, including: a failure in a service provided by regional health authorities, district health authorities and family health services authorities; a failure by one of these authorities to provide a service which it is a function of the authority to provide; and maladministration connected with any other action taken on behalf of one of the authorities. At the end of an investigation by the ombudsman, the complainant will be provided with a copy of the final report, which will also be served upon the authority involved. It is also highly likely that the local Community Health Council will have copies of all ombudsman reports relating to their area, and these should normally be available for inspection at the CHC's offices.

The Audit Commission. The Audit Commission is a government financial watchdog set up in 1983 to appoint auditors to all health authorities, NHS trusts and local government authorities in England and Wales, and to promote studies to encourage economy, efficiency and effectiveness in the NHS and in local government. However, the National Association of Community Health Councils in England and Wales reported in 1991 that the findings of investigations carried out by the Audit Commission into hospitals, health authorities and hospital trusts were being kept secret simply because no provision had been made for their publication. When the Commission conducts a health audit, a general report is published, but this does not name the individual hospitals or units. This audit is then followed by detailed studies of individual hospitals. A full statement of findings is then sent to the hospital executive and a separate summary statement to the health authority or trust members. Confused? If so, then contact the Association of Community Health Councils in England and Wales for an update on the rules, or the Audit Commission at Nicholson House, Lime Kiln Close, Stoke Gifford, Bristol, BS12 6SU. Telephone: 0117-236757. The Audit Commission publishes a useful publications list, available from its Bristol office, which includes such titles as *Code of Audit Practice for Local Authorities and the NHS in England and Wales* (free).

Chapter eight

Voluntary Sector Organizations

THE voluntary sector is a loose term that covers thousands of charities, pressure groups, non-profit-making organizations and foundations that exert considerable social and political pressure throughout the country – including our town halls and parliament – and which control billions of pounds in grants and donations each year. Such bodies include think-tanks, research bodies, educational trusts, religious organizations, campaigning groups and philanthropic foundations. They range from such household names as the Nuffield Foundation, Oxfam and the National Council for Civil Liberties, through to small, local groups that might just be a handful of individuals who meet on an occasional basis to discuss a specific subject. Most of these will, of course, be legitimate organizations that operate fully within the law and provide a range of invaluable services to the public, particularly to disadvantaged sections of the community. And they also include small *ad hoc* campaigning groups that are involved in non-party political quests, such as campaigning against the export of live veal calves or the development of new road schemes through the otherwise unspoilt Green Belt. But the voluntary sector can also include some unscrupulous individuals, dodgy political or quasi-political groups, and the downright corrupt. Also within this sector are a range of organizations that provide a fascinating insight into the way that power is concentrated and manipulated within our society. To begin with, though, it is worth once again drawing up a checklist that will help with the strategic planning of an investigation, and also help assess the precise reasons for undertaking it. It might include the following points:

- What are the given aims and objectives of this organization, and does it have a constitution or other governing document that has been published?

- Who are the members of the main governing committee or board of management that has executive control over the organization?

- Within that structure, who are the main dominant individuals behind the running of the organization? For example, who are the secretary and chairperson? And does it employ a key figure such as a director or general secretary to run the organization on a day-to-day basis?

- Who are the organization's individual members and affiliates? Can anyone join, or is there a vetting procedure, such as 'Membership by invitation only'? And what are the membership and affiliation fees?

- What are the organization's various sources of income? Are there just one or two major benefactors? And is it possible to obtain a copy of the organization's accounts?

- What promotional material and publications does the organization produce? Is there a published annual report that contains detailed accounts, a chronology of activities, list of members or supporters, details of committee members and officers and the like? Are there any press cuttings available on the organization's activities?

- Is the organization affiliated to any national or local groups and organizations? Conversely, are any national or local organizations affiliated to the organization under scrutiny? Is there an evolving 'family tree' of interconnected organizations, or a small number of individuals who are active in a range of organizations?

• Does the organization meet regularly, and, if so, where and when? Are meetings open to the public, or is there a strictly members-only policy?

• Is the organization a limited company or registered charity? If so, is the investigation so important at this stage that it would be useful obtaining copies of the Companies House microfiches or the Charity Commissioners' files?

It will be fairly simple to answer these questions for the vast majority of organizations, as a group engaged only in legitimate activities and with nothing to hide will normally be 'transparent' and willing to place information about itself in the public domain. There may be a small minority of groups and organizations, however, that are more difficult to investigate, and in such cases the earlier section on research methodology will be particularly appropriate.

Local groups and organizations. On the whole, voluntary sector groups usually fall into one of two categories: local or national. Local groups usually exist to attract support, new members and donations, and to educate or inform the public. Therefore researching information on such groups is usually a straightforward procedure. The obvious starting place for any such investigation is the tried and tested local reference library which may well have a separate register or file on such groups. This material will often cover local charities, pressure groups, party-political organizations, amenity groups, and those involved in social activities, hobbies and pastimes. It may also contain details of local branches of national organizations such as charities. Some library services now put all this data on to their computer system so that it can be accessed on the computer terminals at each branch library.

A local organization may also be a member of the local Council for Voluntary Service (CVS) which will be an umbrella group for a number of local charities and other service-providers. The principal purpose of a CVS is to negotiate with the local government authorities and health authorities for block grant-aid, so that individual groups avoid having to negotiate their own funding applications in competition with each other. This may also mean that such groups and organizations share other facilities, such as office accommodation, computer systems and meeting rooms.

This is useful information, as shared accommodation might be the source of further intelligence and information on other groups and organizations in the area and, possibly, yield further resources for a hard-up investigative journalist or campaigner. The voluntary sector in any locality will generate its own culture and personalities, and the investigative researcher could well benefit from getting to know such individuals and organizations.

The final point to remember in researching local groups and organizations is simply to try the direct approach: call or write to the outfit and ask them to send you further details and information. Unless it is a paramilitary or terrorist organization, there can be little harm in making such an enquiry – remember the approach made by the local National Council for Civil Liberties group to the Kent Constabulary detailed in Chapter 1.

National groups and organizations. To find out about a national organization, it is possible to send off direct to the organization for background material, or obtain third-party information such as press cuttings and backgrounders, and of course the Companies House records. Many national pressure groups, campaigning organizations, charities and trusts are 'companies limited by guarantee'. This means they are non-profit-making organisations that enjoy all the benefits of limited liability without issuing shares. If the company goes bust, the directors' personal liability is usually limited to £1 each. But it also means that the organization has to file the same mass of information and accounts as any commercial private limited company.

Registered charities. In 1994 there were some 171,000 registered charities in England and Wales with a combined income estimated to be in the region of £11.5 billion. However, the Charity Commissioners – the government's official charities' watchdog – investigated 864 charities for fraud or irregularity during the year. A total of 12,600 new charities registered during 1994 – almost three times the number which did so during the previous year – as 3,326 women's institutes, 2,736 pre-school playgroups and 1,172 parent-teacher associations complied with new rules requiring registration of all such groups with an annual income in excess of £1,000. The total number of continuing investigations into charities at the end of 1994 was in the region of 900, involving among other things maladministration, fund-raising abuse, deliberate malpractice, and improper political activities. The Charity Commissioners maintain files on every registered charity, and these are open to public inspection without fee. Each file includes a 'governing document' which is usually a trust deed or constitution setting out the organization's broad aims and objectives; the charity's original application to register; and copies of recent accounts. These documents will reveal the charity's stated activities, sources of funding and the membership of its management committee or board of management. The Charity Commissioners publish a range of leaflets including, usefully, leaflet RE4: 'The Central Register of Charities' which details how its own records are organized. This, and a copy of the Charity Commissioners' list of some 40 explanatory leaflets on all aspects of charity administration and law, is obtainable free by sending a large stamped and self-addressed envelope to: Charity Commissioners, St Alban's House, 57–60 Haymarket, London, SW1Y 4QX. It is possible to order copies of the Charity Commissioners file on a specific charity by post. It is worth checking the procedure, and current copying and postage fees, with them by telephoning 0171–210 3000 or 0171–210 4477.

Friendly societies. Friendly societies include some 10,000 non-profit-making bodies that exist to provide specific services to their members – unlike charities, which provide their services for the broader public good. Friendly societies often include building societies, co-operatives, housing societies, provident saving schemes, Working Men's Clubs (*sic*), and other organizations registered under the Industrial and Provident Societies Acts 1965–78. These bodies are required to file returns and accounts with the Registrar of Friendly Societies on formation and then annually. Most friendly societies will also be 'companies limited by guarantee'. Although a range of basic documents are available for public inspection at the main offices of the Registrar of Friendly Societies, there is no facility for arranging a postal search. Therefore, if the friendly society is a limited company, more information will be available on the Companies House records. Otherwise, for further information on inspecting a friendly society's records, contact the Registrar of Friendly Societies at 13 Great Marlborough Street, London, W1V 2AX. Telephone 0171–437 9992.

Churches and religious organizations. Such organizations may fulfil a predominantly spiritual role, but many of them also operate major property and investment portfolios. They are also hugely influential in many of the decision-making bodies of our society such as parliament – the House of Lords has a number of prominent bishops and archbishops sitting as ex-officio members. And the Church Commissioners, as has already been reported, control a multibillion pound portfolio of commercial and industrial property, stocks and shares, and other worldly investments. Many other religious organizations have a quasi-commercial structure. The Worldwide Church of God, for example, is the Pasadena-based evangelical organization that each month publishes more than 7 million copies of *The Plain Truth*. Its operation in the United Kingdom is both a registered charity and a limited company, and its trading subsidiaries include Ambassador Press Limited and Ambassador College (UK) Limited, the latter of which operates a mainframe computer that is registered both in the *Computer-Users Year Book* and on the *Data Protection Register*. Therefore such organizations can be investigated in much the same way as any other. The following is a list of specialist directories and year-books that are often stocked in public libraries: *Baptist Union Directory, Buddhist Directory, Catholic Directory, Church of England Yearbook, Church of Scotland Yearbook, Crockford's Clerical Directory, Fellowship of Independent Evangelical Churches Yearbook, Friends' Book of Meetings Yearbook* (Quakers), *Garlick's Methodist Directory, General Assembly of Unitarian and Free Churches Directory, Jewish Yearbook, Salvation Army Yearbook, The Good Churches Guide, United Reformed Church Yearbook* and the *Zionist Yearbook*. Each usually provides detailed information on the finances, organization and personnel involved in the organization.

Directory of British Associations. This is the definitive directory of volutary organizations in the UK, with more than 8,000 listings of national societies and associations including trade associations, scientific and technical societies, professional institutions, learned societies, research organizations, chambers of commerce, trade unions, religious groups, political organizations and quangos. There are hundreds of cross-references that locate organizations that have changed their names or merged with others, including a category listed as 'unverified and lost associations'. It provides information on fields of interest and activity, membership, affiliations, activities and publications.

Councils, committees and boards. This is also from CBD Research Limited and lists the thousands of consultative and advisory bodies in the United Kingdom. Its entry in CBD's catalogue states that its purpose is to ' ... provide information on bodies whose common factor is that they bring together, by invitation or appointment, groups of experts or representatives of other organisations, for the purposes of advising the government or public authorities, exercising regulatory, investigatory, administrative or executive functions in the public interest, reviewing problems of public concern, or co-ordinating common interests of public authorities or other organisations'. It provides detailed information on each of the thousands of bodies listed.

Centres and bureaux. This is a further directory from CBD Research that lists hundreds of local and specialist advisory organizations and help-lines, from the Advisory Centre for Education, to the Women's Reproductive Rights Information Centre. It lists such information as postal address, names of principal staff, when and by whom established, sources of finance, objects, activities, services to the public, publications, and the like.

The Henderson Top 2,000 Charities. Rather than spending the time and trouble of searching the Charities Commissioners files or Companies House microfiches, first take a look at *The Henderson Top 2,000 Charities* year-book. This is a substantial directory of 1,200 pages that provides details on trustees and staff; five years comparative figures for income, expenditure and funds; league table of charities listed by legacy, voluntary and investment income; grant makers, the causes they support and how much funding they give; and details of auditors, legal and financial advisers, investment managers and their charity clients.

Other directories. A wide range of directories is published on charities, grant-making trusts and company giving, and many of these are stocked by public libraries. *The Charities Digest*, published by the Charities Aid Foundation, lists some 1,200 charities in the UK, and also details the work of the Charities Commissioners, the

Central Register and the Official Custodian of Charities, and provides an outline of charity law, registration and regulation. *The Directory of Grant-Making Trusts*, also published by the Charities Aid Foundation, is an 'encyclopaedia of treasure-houses' that details around 3,000 grant-making trusts, ranging from household names such as the Wellcome Trust and the Rowntree Foundation, to local trusts with only a few thousand pounds to give in annual awards. It provides a series of cross-referenced subject-based indexes on which funding is given. There are also now several major publications, such as *A Guide to Company Giving*, which analyse the charitable grants and awards made each year by the major companies and the corporations.

A case study: freemasonry

It is useful to look at a specimen investigation into a multi-million pound voluntary sector organization that operates at both national and local level and has a network of thousands of local branches with an estimated national membership of around half a million. The subject chosen here, freemasonry, also attracts considerable public interest because of its inherent secrecy, and this gives us the opportunity to look at ways in which factual information can be obtained to challenge that secrecy. It also allows us to illustrate the distinction between fact and fiction – these tend to get confused in controversial subjects such as freemasonry – which has the added benefit of eliminating conspiracy theories and converting them into conspiracy facts.

Unlike many voluntary sector organizations, freemasonry does not admit anyone who simply fills in an application form and pays an annual subscription fee. A prospective freemason has to be proposed as a member by at least two existing members of the brotherhood, and the term 'brotherhood' also implies that more than half the population, women, are excluded from membership of the masonic fellowship.

So we have to rely upon third-party information from a variety of sources. A very good starting point would be to obtain copies of the two definitive published works on the subject: *The Brotherhood* by Stephen Knight (Grafton, 1985) and *Inside the*

Brotherhood – Further Secrets of the Freemasons by Martin Short (Grafton, 1989). These two investigative writers used empirical means to obtain their information, which principally involved the placing of small advertisements in newspapers and magazines asking for freemasons to come forward – anonymously if they preferred – with information. The tactic of placing the small ads had worked, and provided the necessary background information for the detailed investigations to proceed. Both books were stunning successes and sold tens of thousands of copies. For the first time there had been a major exposé of the secret society of freemasons, and Short's book substantially added to, and updated, the pioneering work undertaken by the late Stephen Knight. Needless to say, both books attracted considerable media attention, and lists of the names of prominent freemasons appeared in such outlets as the diary column of *The Guardian* (which published a regular item entitled 'Your Freemasons Tonight'!) Even now these two books are basic sourcebooks on freemasonic matters.

But there was one other source of information that even exceeded these two tomes – *The Masonic Year Book* – if only one knew where to obtain access to a copy. The trouble with this book is that it was published only for internal consumption; it would not be possible to order a copy through a bookshop. However, a small group of journalists knew that one public library in the heart of London had a copy on its shelves. That library is Westminster Central Reference Library – between Leicester Square and the National Gallery on Trafalgar Square. The reason the masonic hierarchy allowed Westminster Library service to stock a copy was so that any mason arriving in central London and in need of help would know where to go in the first instance. This was an open secret that Fleet Street hacks were prepared to play along with in return for the opportunity to delve into one of the most revealing books on the subject.

This secret can now be revealed because the masonic fraternity scored an own-goal in the provision of this information when a *Guardian* journalist, Ian Katz, made a telephone call to the masons' headquarters in Covent Garden. At the time, leading freemasons had been protesting that freemasonry was *not* a secret society – merely a society with secrets. Ian Katz had written in some depth about the subject and was, of course, aware of the Westminster Library copy of the *Masonic Year Book*. As he was interviewing the Grand Secretary, Commander Michael Higham, he asked if he could buy a copy of the *Masonic Year Book*. After all, freemasonry is not a secret society – it is just a society with secrets – and there is even a copy of the year-book in Westminster's main reference library. The Grand Secretary had little option but to agree that, yes, copies of the *Masonic Year Book* were available for purchase by the public at Freemasons' Hall for £10. Another great triumph for campaigning journalism. Freemasons' Hall, incidentally, is located in Great Queen Street, Covent Garden, London, WC2B 5AZ. Telephone: 0171–831 9811.

The Masonic Year Book is around 900 pages long and packed with fascinating information. Its list of contents runs something like this: Meetings of the Grand Lodge; Grand Officers Appointments and Promotions; Provincial Grand Masters, Chronological list of; District Grand Masters, Chronological list of; Grand Inspectors, Chronological list of; Orders of Service to Masonry, List of Holders of; Representatives of other Grand Lodges; Board of General Purposes; Appeals Court; Scrutineers; Grand Secretary's Office; Lodges, Numerical list of; Lodges, Alphabetical list of; Lodges Diary – London; Lodges, Alphabetical list of – Provincial; Towns where Provincial Lodges meet; Provincial Grand Lodges, Details of; Provincial Grand Secretaries, Addresses of; District Grand Lodges, Details of; District Grand Secretaries, Addresses of; Grand Inspectorates, Details of; Grand Officers, Alphabetical list of; Grand Officers, Prefixes; Abbreviation of Masonic Ranks; Statistics; Accounts; Outstanding Masonic Events; Aims and Relationships of the Craft; Basic Principles for Grand Lodge Recognition; Grand Lodges, Recognised; Prestonian Lectureship; Royal Arch; Convocations of Grand Chapter; Grand Scribe E's Office; Grand Officers, Alphabetical list of; Grand Officers – Appointment and Promotions; Grand Superintendents in Provinces, Chronological List of; Grand Superintendents in Districts, Chronological list of; Grand Chapter Committee; Chapters; Provincial Grand Chapters; Details of; Provincial Grand Scribes, Addresses of; District Grand Chapters, Details of; Grand Inspectorates, Details of; Calendar Notes and Calendars; Great Queen Street Diary; Grand Lodge Library and

Museum; Royal Masonic Benevolent Institution; Royal Masonic Hospital; Masonic Foundation for the Aged and the Sick; Masonic Trust for Girls and Boys; Masonic Housing Association; New Masonic Samaritan Fund; and Grand Charity.

A copy of the *Masonic Year Book*, therefore, would be invaluable to anyone undertaking detailed research into the masonic network. One interesting observation: the two following entries appear in the *London Business and Services Telephone Directory*: Honourable Fraternity of Ancient Freemasons (Members), 68 Great Cumberland Place, London, W1H 7FD. Telephone 0171-723 9526; and Supreme Council 33rd Degree, 10 Duke Street, London, SW1Y 6BS. Telephone 0171-930 1606. Neither of these addresses appears in any of the above-mentioned publications, which just goes to show how elusive is this body that is 'not a secrect society – just a society with secrets'.

The key data to be gleaned from the *Masonic Year Book* are details of the thousands of provincial masonic lodges around the country, including details of when and where they meet. In London, for example, there are 1,700 masonic lodges and over 700 grand chapters. And the name of a lodge or chapter often says a great deal about its membership. The following are examples of lodges in London: (with lodge number in brackets): Authors (3456); Bank of England (263); Barbican (8494); Centre Point (7866); Certified Accountants (7582); Chartered Architects (3244); City University (7962); Guildhall (3116); Houshold Brigade (2614); Lloyds (5673); London Mayors (3560); Moorfields (4949); National Artillery (2578); National Westminster (3647); Old Etonian (4500); Portcullis (6085); Public Schools Installed Masters (9077); Radio Fraternity (8040); Royal Air Force (7335); Royal Albert Hall (2986); Royal Dental Hospital (7099); Savoy (8356); Spitalfields (4836); Telephone (3301); Temple Bar (1728); University of London (2033); and Whitehall (3020). It is not unknown for keen mason-spotters and journalists to stake out such meetings in order to identify leading masonic figures. But information is easily obtained on local freemasons by using less strenuous methods.

Take, for example, the masonic structure in Kent. The 1992 *Masonic Year Book* shows that the Provincial Grand Master for East Kent – the most senior mason in the area – is one John A. Porter

TD, DL. His entry in *Who's Who* shows that he is a prominent local estate agent and a director of several building societies, has a military background, was president of the Gravesend Conservative Association from 1965 until 1977, was appointed a magistrate in 1952, and is a commissioner of taxes and former president of Kent County Cricket Club. A decent and law-abiding man – and a true Establishment man. The same can be said for Provincial Grand Master for West Kent, one Simon F.N. Waley. His entry in *Who's Who* shows him to be better known as His Honour Judge Felix Waley QC: Charterhouse, Oxford, the Royal Navy, Middle Temple barrister, Court Recorder, Crown Court Judge and former Conservative councillor and prospective parliamentary candidate.

A closer examination of the local masonic structure for the Medway Towns of Kent – Rochester, Chatham and Gillingham – shows how the power and influence of such figures filters down very rapidly at a local level. At least four masonic lodges in the Medway Towns – King's Navy (lodge no. 2901), White Ensign of Gillingham (4180), Royal Engineers Chatham (4465) and General Gordon (4292) – are directly linked with the armed forces. The local city council has a lodge of its own (City of Rochester, lodge no. 7941) and so do the police (Manor of Chatham, lodge no. 4688; and Manor of Gillingham, lodge no. 3983). The Medway Towns telephone directory lists three masonic clubs in the area: Chatham and District Freemasons Hall and Club Limited; the Gillingham Hall and Club Limited; and the Rochester Masonic Hall and Club Limited. As each is a limited company, a complete set of Companies House records is available, and these will also list the names of all directors of the company and also its shareholders. One will soon be able to build up a detailed picture of the *Who's Who* of local freemasons by using one or two fairly inexpensive sources of information. An obscure and now out-of-print publication called *The Secret Society of the Freemasons in Bradford* (published by a community group called 1 in 12 and based at 31 Manor Row, Bradford 1) detailed an excellent investigation that linked certain key members of the local masonic fraternity with a company that purchased a plot of land from the local council just before the council announced a development project in the area. This caused the value of neighbouring land, including the plot purchased by the masonic company, to sky-rocket overnight. The publication of this investigation by local community activists was certainly a clever and shrewd piece of work.

Whatever one might feel about freemasons, it is the case that this fraternity is a concentration of social and political power involving a range of key institutions in our society. The *Masonic Year Book* lists prominent members of the judiciary, Church of England, the armed forces, industry, the professions, the aristocracy, and other institutions as being prominent members of the masonic fraternity. Even when they are acting fully within the law, it is in the public interest to know exactly who they are, and how the various individuals and institutions are linked. And the same can be said for most of the voluntary sector.

Chapter nine

Law and Order

The police

EACH police force in the country is overseen by a police authority, and outside of London (where the Metropolitan Police Authority is the Home Office) the police authority is either a committee of the county council, or a joint local government committee (as, for example, the Thames Valley Constabulary and the Avon and Somerset Constabulary). Either way, the Police Authority is subject to local government law, including the Local Government (Access to Information) Act 1985, as detailed in Chapter 6. In practice, a constabulary's activities are divided into two separate areas: operational, which is largely regulated and controlled by the Police Act 1964 and therefore a matter of negotiation between the chief constable and the Home Secretary; and 'administration and supply', which is the responsibility of the local police authority via the county council.

But this division of responsibility does not prevent investigative research from being used to obtain detailed information on the operational aspect of a police force. The same Local Government (Access to Information) Act 1985 applies to the police as to any other facet of local government activity and, indeed, the 1985 Act does not even distinguish between the police authority and other council committees. There are therefore no specific confidentiality clauses that relate to police work.

An example of the way in which local government law can be used to investigate police operational activities is a shrewd piece of investigative journalism undertaken by a small radical community newspaper called the *City Enquirer* back in the early 1980s. As we saw in Chapter 6, under the Local Government Finance Act 1982, the public is given a brief period of some two weeks at the time of the audit of a council's accounts to inspect the accounts and ' ... all books, deeds, contracts, bills, vouchers and receipts relating thereto'.

The editor of the *City Enquirer*, one Mike Donne, went along to the Greater Manchester Council during the designated period and inspected the documents relating to expenditure by the Greater Manchester police force. After much burrowing, he discovered an invoice relating to the purchase of two machine pistols – a transaction that would have been far more controversial in the early 1980s than today. The story duly ran in the *City Enquirer*, was then picked up by the now defunct investigative magazine *The Leveller*, and then subsequently appeared as a front-page exclusive story in the *Observer*.

During the course of his investigation, Mike Donne also came across documents relating to Greater Manchester's emergency planning arrangements which at the time provided evidence of a massive increase in war preparations, such as the number of emergency planning personnel, and spending on the region's expanded emergency war headquarters. Invoices from the Easingwold Home Defence College in Yorkshire provided lists of officers and councillors who had been on courses on the preparations for nuclear war, and brief descriptions of the courses themselves. Evidently the administration and supply aspect of a police force – often administered by the county council – can actually tell the investigative researcher a great deal about the operational side of the local constabulary. Therefore the investigator needs a thorough understanding of the mechanisms of local government and the tactics outlined in Chapter 6 for obtaining local government documents.

Police and Constabulary Almanac

This is the main directory of police forces in the United Kingdom and also contains details of fire brigades and ambulance services, civil defence, and courts of law. Curiously, the *Almanac* has printed on its front cover the caveat: 'This almanac is obtainable direct from the publisher only'. The publisher in question is R. Hazell and Co, P.O. Box 39, Henley-on-Thames, RG9 5UA. Telephone Nettlebed (01491) 641018. Fortunately, given that the *Almanac* costs £22, it appears to be stocked by most major reference libraries. It contains detailed sections on the Home Office Police Department including the C5 Division Drugs Branch, Scientific Research and Development Branch, Police Requirement Support Service, Central Planning Units, Police National Computer Organisation, Forensic Science Service, Her Majesty's Inspectors of Constabulary, Police Colleges and Training Centres, National Identification Bureau, National Criminal Intelligence Service, Regional Crime Squads, Interpol, the Crown Prosecution Service, Serious Fraud Office, Police Complaints Authority, Association of Chief Police Officers, Superintendents' Association, Police Federation, etc. It then provides a detailed directory of each police force in the country, including such gems as the Royal Parks Constabulary, Royal Botanic Gardens Constabulary, and the UK Atomic Energy Authority Constabulary, and an organizational breakdown of each force. This includes a list of senior officers working in each constabulary, and even direct-line telephone numbers. The *Almanac* also gives an outline of the policing arrangements for each port, harbour, dock, tunnel and airport, plus details of the policing and investigatory agencies inside the Post Office, British Telecom, the BBC and Customs and Excise.

Chief Constables' annual reports

Most Chief Constables and Police Authorities publish an annual report which is very often a glitzy piece of public relations material. But it should also contain useful information on the activities of the constabulary and its officers. For example, the 1993 annual report of the Acting Commissioner of the City of London Police is an 80-page glossy document with sections on the Special Branch, Criminal Investigation Department, Fraud Investigation Department, Scientific Support Unit, Tactical Firearms Group, Counter Terrorist Search Team, Command Structures, etc. The report also contains 19 pages of statistics, including accounts and tables of personnel levels (from which useful detailed information can be derived), and several schedules of what are described as 'interesting cases'. However, the report also contains its fair share of bland promotional material: the presentation of awards; sporting achievements; letters of appreciation; a photograph of 'PC Robin Fisher receiving a Community Police Officer of the Year certificate from Prime Minister John Major' and the like. Still, the document is well worth spending some time over, and the local annual report should be in main reference libraries.

Data Protection Register

The Data Protection Act 1984 requires data users (that's the people who operate computer systems) to supply data subjects (that's people whose details appear on computers – invariably the public at large) with a copy of their own computer files. Part of the process of enabling data subjects to apply for this information is the inspection of entries on the Data Protection Register, a public register containing details of the categories and types of information held about data subjects on each computer system. It is this public register that often provides useful information on the activites of a data user such as the police. When the system was first set up, copies of the Data Protection Register were held on microfiche at every reference library in the country. However, since several million computers are now registered, it has become impossible to maintain the microfiche register system: copies of entries on the register are available directly from the Office of the Data Protection Registrar. Obtaining copies of entries from the Data Protection Register is a straightforward procedure. Simply telephone the Registrar's office on (01625) 535711 and ask for the Registration Department. Then give the Registration Department the name of the police force for which you would like copies of the Data Protection Register entries, and a few days later the print-outs will arrive in the post. And there is no fee for the service.

An example of a police entry on the Data Protection Register relates to the Police National Computer – entry number E0576126 – which lists 63 separate categories of information. Included in these categories are: 'personal details; habits; personality; character; current marriage or partnership; lifestyle; membership of voluntary and charitable bodies; membership of committees; mental health record; sexual life; political opinions; political party membership; support for pressure groups; religious beliefs; other beliefs; uncategorised information', etc. The information detailing the sources of that data, and the individuals and organizations to whom it is disclosed, is equally worrying. They include: 'Credit reference agencies (source and disclosure); debt collecting and tracing agencies (source); private detective agencies and security organisations (source and disclosure); voluntary, charitable, religious organisations or associations (source); political organisations (source); traders in personal information (source).'

The way this information is presented in the register entries is usually quite self-explanatory, although the Registration Department is most helpful and can advise on any problems with interpreting entries on the register. The Office of the Data Protection Registrar publishes a range of free leaflets on the use and abuse of the Data Protection Act 1984, and these are available from Wycliffe House, Water Lane, Wilmslow, Cheshire, SK9 5AF, telephone (01625) 535777.

Press cuttings

The police is a favoured topic of press and media coverage – and not just for the criminal investigations they undertake. In the last ten or fifteen years numerous police forces have been the subject of press scrutiny over false arrests, planting of evidence, assaults on suspects, disputes between senior officers, massaged clear-up statistics, use of informants and supergrasses, and other controversies. Therefore, once again, check with the library service local to the police force in question to establish if a file of press cuttings is kept on the activities of the local constabulary.

Serious Fraud Office

Occasionally the British government comes up with what looks like a good idea on ways of clamping down on crime, and following the range of high profile fraud cases that took place in the late eighties and early nineties, the government set up the Serious

Fraud Office (SFO). Unfortunately the SFO was not very good at its job, and in early 1995 it even looked as though it might be closed down when the press announced that one of its rare successes – the case involving the Guinness bid for Distillers – was to be referred to the Court of Appeal. This was because it emerged that a secret City tribunal had already heard the case against Guinness and cleared it of any wrongdoing. Despite this, though, the Serious Fraud Office does publish an annual report which details types of fraud investigated, case results, appeals, progress of cases, use of statutory powers, disclosure of information, management of investigations, policy on the acceptance of cases, and policy on prosecutions. It also features two detailed appendices: the aims and objectives of the Serious Fraud Office; and cases worked on during the year. An interesting read.

Defence

It could be argued that the most difficult type of research to carry out relates to the world of defence, but this is not necessarily the case. Bear in mind the case cited in the introduction to this book about the memorandum from a senior official in the Ministry of Defence to government ministers that was forced into the open at the Matrix Churchill trial: 'Much of this information can be declassified, since all this will take is someone like an investigative journalist to pull together the threads ... '. But where might one start an investigation to pull together those sensitive threads?

The market leaders in information on defence matters are the Jane's Information Group (Sentinel House, Brighton Road, Coulsdon, Surrey, CR5 2NH. Telephone: 0181–763 1030). 'It is the leading international defence and aerospace information provider, and a major supplier of data to clients from industry and governments worldwide', according to its publications catalogue. In fact the Jane's Information Group publications catalogue for 1988, the year when the arms-to-Iraq trade was at its peak, gives an insight into the detailed information that was in the public domain and available to 'Industry and governments worldwide'. The catalogue provides the following salient descriptions of some of their more obscure annuals, periodicals and services:

'*Jane's Security and CO-IN Equipment 1989–90*: The 2nd edition gives you complete information on the equipment used by military, paramilitary, and security forces in internal security and counter-insurgency operations. It describes equipment and is fully illustrated.'

'*Jane's Strategic Weapon Systems*: This new product discusses the political and technical aspects of offensive and defensive strategic systems around the world. Included are treaty details, constraints, compliance and future prospects. Three updates will be provided automatically.'

'*World Ordnance Inventory and Forecast 1989/90*: This annual survey covers 100 countries, detailing current inventories of ordnance, force structure analysis, procurement histories and future acquisitions. It includes towed and self-propelled artillery, armoured vehicles, armaments, mortars, artillery ammunition, anti-tank weapons, automatic cannons and rocket launchers.'

The most revealing entry in the catalogue, however, refers to Jane's Information Services ' ... which is able to provide you with exclusive research and analysis on any aerospace, defence, or transport subject'. The entry reads: 'Jane's Information Services undertakes customised, specifically targeted Market Research Studies for clients when published sources do not provide sufficient information. This service is authoritative, impartial and completely confidential, and draws on the unrivalled information sources available to the Jane's Information Group. Our clients include *defence ministries, government agencies* and numerous companies worldwide' (emphasis added).

And the Jane's Information Group publications themselves are a real eye-opener. For example, *Jane's Armour and Artillery 1994–95* (fifteenth edition, 800 pages) contains detailed technical data, plans and photographs of tanks, reconnaissance vehicles, armoured personnel carriers, armoured fighting vehicle families, tank destroyers, self-propelled guns and howitzers, towed anti-tank guns and howitzers, multiple rocket launchers, coastal artillery guns and missiles, armour and artillery weapons. These relate to all manufacturers from around the world, including those from the old Eastern bloc countries.

Jane's Infantry Weapons 1994–95 (twentieth edition, 713 pages) contains details of every conceivable firearm and missile imaginable, plus landing equipment and associated paraphernalia. It includes sections on personal weapons (pistols, sub-machine-guns, rifles and light support weapons); crew-served weapons (machine guns, cannons, anti-tank weapons, mortars, mortar fire-control); ammunition; sighting equipment, etc.

Jane's Military Vehicles and Logistics 1994–95 (fifteenth edition, 755 pages) covers armoured engineer vehicles; recovery vehicles and equipment; bridging systems; mine warfare equipment; transport equipment; miscellaneous equipment (such as water supplies, field hospitals, camouflage equipment and decoys, etc.).

Jane's Fighting Ships 1994–95. (Ninety-seventh edition, 886 pages). Every form of sea-based warfare craft imaginable is detailed in this book, including battleships, submarines, hovercraft, hydrofoils, patrol craft, police launches, and training and survey ships.

Jane's All The World's Aircraft contains 800 pages of data on light aircraft, monoplanes, sailplanes, hang-gliders, areoplane engines, airships, helicopters, and long-distance reconnaissance aircraft, including the new Northrup Grumman B-2A Sprite, and so on.

The 1994 Jane's catalogue also contains a few surprises. It parades a new addition to the Jane's stable, *Jane's Security and Counter Insurgency Equipment 1994–95*, and describes this title as 'The detailed annual guide to equipment used by military, paramilitary and security forces in security and counter-insurgency operations. Up-to-date information on 2,000 items of equipment from over 500 manufacturers worldwide.' It covers firearms, operational equipment (surveillance equipment, rapid entry devices and the like), armour protection, and command, control, communications systems and intelligence for use in riot control. The publication boasts its readership to include ' ... 10,694 military/government readers'. Information obtained by the Jane's Information Group has hit the headlines from time to time. The 1988 edition of *Jane's Military Communications* revealed that the Soviet navy had Extremely Low Frequency (ELF) radio evesdropping equipment built into all its ballistic missile submarines, as well as the Oscar and Charlie class cruise missile submarines. This was news to NATO, which had been experiencing technical problems with its own ELF surveillance capability, and this news made the pages of several serious broadsheet newspapers.

This type of information is largely put together from material that is already in the public domain – manufacturers catalogues, marketing material distributed at trade fairs and the like. Bearing in mind that arms manufacturers are invariably commercial operations that depend upon sales for their existence, it is very difficult to keep all this information secret. After all, British manufacturers of military equipment exported goods valued at a record £5.2 billion in 1993 (75 per cent of which was destined for the Third World). So these companies can be researched in much the same way as any other company.

And that is precisely what the Campaign Against the Arms Trade was set up to do. This is a pressure group founded in 1974 by a broad coalition of groups and individuals to research into the arms industry and it has developed a considerable library on the subject. This includes a wide range of press cuttings, published directories, company brochures and related material on the arms industry. The campaign in turn widely disseminates this information in the form of publications, training seminars and publicity. In 1990 it published an excellent briefing entitled *The Government and the Arms Trade* which was produced in the light of the revelations about the arms-to-Iraq case. It covers the Export of Goods (Control Order) and the licensing system, government secrecy, international conventions, the organization of the arms industry, the internal structure of the Ministry of Defence's Defence Export Services Organisation (DESO), the government's Export Credits Guarantee Department and the like. The campaign's own newsletter provides periodical updates of the arms industry, and its April 1989 edition revealed that some thirteen British companies participated in the First Baghdad International Exhibition for Military Production – a matter overlooked by the national press and broadcast media. The Campaign Against the Arms Trade can be found at 11 Goodwin Street, Finsbury Park, London, N4 3HQ. Telephone 0171–281 0297.

A further publication that provides a fascinating study of the arms industry, and which is an essential read for anyone attempting this type of research, is the *Priate Eye Arms-to-Iraq Special: Not the*

Scott Report which retails at £1.50. Despite its whimsical title, this report by investigative journalists Paul Foot and Tim Laxton pulls together all the material available on the arms-to-Iraq débâcle and merges it with the evidence disclosed at the Scott Inquiry. This has resulted in a very thorough and damning report, the fruit of an exemplary investigative research project.

Military research

Another source of information on military matters is provided by the military research projects that are being undertaken by colleges and universities around the country. As these are public bodies, there is often a wealth of published information on this type of research, given that government departments and companies producing military equipment will often fund such research. So one can dig out a considerable amount of information on the arms industry by simply turning to a few readily accessible publications.

The first of these is the annual report published by each university or college and held in the institution's own library. Although the format will vary from one college to another, it is highly likely that the report will contain a list of all research grants received by the institution during the academic year to which it relates. After all, academic bodies do like to flaunt their successes, and most funders will expect some sort of recognition in the annual report. It is also worth checking back-copies of the report to see if a college or university has a history of receiving research funds from such government departments or companies. Keep an eye open for glaringly suspicious references to 'a government department' or other ambiguously-described organizations that might benefit from a little more research. Whilst you are at the library it is also worth going through files of the college or university newsletter – usually published by the institution's public relations department – for mention of such awards. Most academic bodies publish a regular newsletter, and these often contain little more than self-serving propaganda items about its successes – particularly in the field of fundraising.

Another source of information on research awards is contained in a directory called *Current Research in Britain* which is a multi-volume register of academic research being undertaken throughout the UK. However, its content can be patchy, as the publisher relies on academics themselves to report their research awards, and this may result in the failure to report controversial areas of research. However, a source of such information which is often more reliable is the *Times Higher Education Supplement*, which lists new research grants in its 'Noticeboard' section. Back-copies of this can be scoured for evidence of arms-related reseach. And, of course, sympathetic academics can also be approached for information, as can such pressure groups as Scientists Against Nuclear Arms, or the Medical Campaign Against Nuclear Weapons (0171–272 2020).

Spies and spying

The Cold War is over, the Berlin Wall is down and the paramilitary campaign that has been terrorizing the communities of Northern Ireland has at last come to an end. And yet the British security service, MI5, still conducts its business in extreme secrecy. This was demonstrated in 1995 when this author telephoned the old number of MI5's former offices in Mayfair's Curzon Street. This number had long been in the public domain as the *New Statesman & Society* magazine had reproduced a piece of MI5's headed notepaper back in the early 1980s, which gave its telephone number as 01–491 4488. By 1995, MI5 had given up its Curzon Street offices for the palatial splendour of new headquarters at 12 Millbank in Westminster. On dialling 0171–491 4488, the author heard the following recorded message: 'The number you have dialled has been changed to 0171–828 8688.' Could this be the new spirit of openness, with MI5 making public its telephone number for the first time? Not likely, as it turned out. This information was duly reported in the diary column of the *Guardian* which coyly printed the old number and suggested that anyone wanting the new number should dial the old one themselves and listen to the recorded message. But, some-how, MI5 got wind of this ruse and before copies of the *Guardian* had reached the nation's breakfast tables, the recorded message had been changed to: 'Sorry, the number you have dialled has not been recognised. Please check and try again.' So much then for the Cold War thaw.

However, journalists do occasionally demonstrate a lack of immagination when investigating matters relating to the security services. The Security Services Tribunal was set up by the government under the Security Services Act 1989 following embarrassing disclosures about certain MI5 activities. Although intended to allay fears that MI5 is an out-of-control freelance political operation with right-wing leanings, the tribunal has been widely denounced by civil liberty reformers and journalists alike as the Security Services Act gives it immunity from any legal challenges. Section 5(4) of the 1989 Act states: 'The decisions of the Tribunal and Commissioner ... shall not be questioned in any court.'

But the Security Services Tribunal has also suffered from severe bouts of shyness. When approached by an *Observer* journalist in 1990, the tribunal's Chairman was unable to tell the reporter the whereabouts of its offices. Asked about its postal address, Lord Justice Stuart Smith said that he was 'not sure offhand', and when pressed he suggested that it might be 'care of the Home Office,' and that 'you will probably find it in the telephone book'. However, the tribunal is not listed in the telephone directory. But the *Observer* investigation resulted in its gleefully announcing the address of the Security Service Tribunal as PO Box 18, London, SE1 OLT, although the paper was unable to give the telephone number. The *Observer* could, however, have identified and published the address of the building in which the tribunal is housed – right down to the room number. The basis of such research is the fact that Post Office boxes are not considered secret; they officially exist for administrative convenience only. A quick call to the local sorting office for that PO box address, in this case the Royal Mail Sorting Office in Southwark, would soon establish that the destination address for PO Box 18 is Room G. 103, Block D, St Christopher House, 80–112 Southwark Street, London, SE1. And that enquiry would also reveal that the same office is used by the Interception of Communications Tribunal which operates from PO Box 44. Although the telephone number of the Security Services Tribunal is not in the phone book, directory inquiries was able to help by pointing out that the Interception of Communications Tribunal is listed under 'Tribunal,

Interception of Communications.' The telephone number given, which is also the current number for the Security Services Tribunal, is 0171–273 4096. The moral of this investigation is simple: secrecy is largely in the eye of the beholder. No doubt the Security Service Tribunal and Interception of Communications Tribunal use a PO box because they believe it to be a confidential facility. Not at all; Post Office box numbers are subject to public scrutiny – including scrutiny by *Observer* journalists, if only they knew where to look.

Further evidence of the truism that 'secrecy is largely in the eye of the beholder' has been provided time and again by the publishers of an alternative magazine with the unlikely name of *Lobster*. This title was set up in 1983 by two researchers, Robin Ramsay and Stephen Dorril, and covers a wide range of issues relating to the security service MI5 and secret intelligence service MI6. In May 1989 it published a special report entitled *Who's Who in the British Secret State*, which detailed the careers of thousands of suspected and actual British intelligence officers. Ramsay and Dorril did this by scouring the pages of numerous books on the security services and painstakingly collating this detailed information. The editors of *Lobster* point out that the material contained in this *Who's Who* is not in itself conclusive evidence of the status of the subjects, but should only be used as a starting point for further research. Thus, their experience confirms the point made by the American reporters in the introduction to this book – a point reiterated by the famous duo Bob Woodward and Carl Bernstein – that much investigative research and journalism is straightforward methodical research obtained by poring over a variety of seemingly dull documents. *Lobster* magazine is acknowledged prime source of material on the security services and can be contacted at 214 Westbourne Avenue, Hull, HU5 3JB.

Another organization that studies and collates data on the security services and related matters is a charity called Statewatch. The organization is based on the *Statewatch* bulletin, which comes out every two months and provides news, information and analysis on such matters as covert MI5 operations, shoot-to-kill allegations, the Police National Computer No.2, and other matters that too often do not gain widespread press coverage. It describes itself as ' ... the journal that is monitoring what is happening in the UK and across Europe – the emergence of the European state, the changes being incorporated at a national level, and their effect on people's rights. It is an indispensable source of information for lawyers, journalists, students and lecturers, researchers, policymakers, trade unionists and community groups.' Statewatch also operates an on-line database of its extensive library of material. Details are obtainable from Statewatch, Freepost, London, N16 OBR. Telephone 0181–802 1882; Fax 0181–880 1727.

Few individual researchers will undertake their own empirical research into security service matters, as by far the best material to have emerged on the subject has surfaced as a result of legal proceedings – such as the Matrix Churchill case or the prosecutions of civil servants like Clive Ponting – but occasionally the press receives leaked documents that provide a fascinating insight into the world of security and intelligence. This happened to Dublin-based *An Phoblacht (Republican News)* which in 1989 received a copy of two lengthy MI5 documents on a joint British/German intelligence proposal to recruit members of the Irish community in continental Europe to work as MI5 agents. The lengthy documents were published in full in the 19 October 1989 edition of *An Phoblacht*, risking legal action by the British authorities. But the British government apparently took the view that it would probably score another own-goal along the lines of the *Spycatcher* affair if it took legal action against the newspaper. Nevertheless, the 19 October 1989 edition of the Republican newspaper provides a rare opportunity to see how the security services organize themselves operationally.

One final source of information on security service matters is the plethora of books published by 'insiders' and others with a unique view of the world of intelligence. But a word of warning: the majority of these books are published with the implied consent of the security services as they serve a useful black-propaganda and disinformation role. For example, in *Spycatcher*, the late Peter Wright demonstrated an amazing capacity to recall conversations that took place decades earlier in such detail that he could quote verbatim what was said. He could even recall aspects of the speaker's body language and facial expressions. The only way that such details can be recalled with clarity after such a period is by being committed to paper at the time. And an officer of the security services would raise a great deal of suspicion if he or she were to keep such detailed diaries of all events relating to his or her job. Many of these books can be seen as little more than unofficial vehicles of propaganda for the security services. Bear in mind that the security services have themselves been engaged in major disinformation campaigns in the past. Books such as *The Wilson Plot* by David Leigh (Heinemann Mandarin, 1989) and *The Silent Conspiracy: Inside the Intelligence Services in the 1990s* by Stephen Dorril (Heinemann, 1993) are reliable accounts of such campaigns and are essential reading for anyone who is planning to undertake research on the subject.

Chapter ten

The Media

THE many newspapers, magazines, and radio and television stations that make up the media in this country are themselves very powerful institutions that play an important role in our society, and their influence is likely to grow as the number of broadcast stations continues to expand. Added to this are the huge developments that are currently taking place on the so-called multimedia 'information super-highway' such as the electronic mail network, cyberspace and peripherals such as CD-ROM. Given that a newspaper can ruin a public figure's career overnight, or help bring a political party to power (as happened in the United Kingdom in 1979), then a media organization might well form a subject for research. For example, who owns your local newspaper, and what are the political views of its proprietor? Which specialist periodical is the most likely to have published detailed articles on a specific subject? And which is the parent company that owns a particular ITV regional television station?

However, most newspapers and broadcasters – with the exclusion of the British Broadcasting Corporation – are themselves limited companies, and as such can be researched in the same way as any other company. But the output of media institutions, such as press cuttings, articles, television and radio programmes, can be of immense use to the researcher. Much of this information is detailed in a range of professional directories that are frequently stocked by the larger public reference and specialist libraries.

Benn's Media Directory. This is a substantial multi-volume directory that is probably the most comprehensive guide to the media both at home and overseas. It lists every newspaper title, periodical and broadcast station in the United Kingdom. It provides cross-references that show the parent companies and the titles or stations that they each own or control. Each entry provides a list of the directors, senior executive and editorial staff employed by the title or station. There are entries for local newspapers classified by county; periodicals; free-distribution newspapers; media directories and other reference serials; classified index of news agencies and other business and editorial services to the media industry; and details of the entire BBC structure and independent broadcasting organizations. Benn's also provides a media subscription service BEMIS – Benn's Editorial Media Information Service – which will answer basic queries about titles over the telephone without charge, or will quote for more detailed research. The BEMIS service is available to any purchaser of the *Benn's Media Directory* and may be available through your main local reference library.

Willing's Press Guide. This provides a comprehensive list of more than 12,000 daily, Sunday, county and local newspapers published in the United Kingdom and Republic of Ireland, plus periodicals and annuals. The guide publishes details of frequency of publication; address, telephone and fax numbers; circulation figures; cover price; editor; advertising director; circulation director; publisher or holding company; and also covers key overseas newspapers and periodicals. It has a number of indexes including: classified index; town-by-town guide of newspaper titles published in the UK and Republic of Ireland; and an alphabetical list of magazine and periodical publishers and their titles.

Writers' and Artists' Yearbook. This is a very useful paperback that publishes a large selection of newspaper and magazine publishers; BBC and independent radio and television stations; book publishers; literary agents; news agencies and syndication services. It also has useful sections on libel law; taxation; welfare rights for the writer; copyright; writing for the European Community; desk-top publishing; self-publishing; picture research; preparing and submitting manuscripts; books, research and reference sources for the writer, etc. This is an essential guide for investigative researchers who are planning in due course to get into print with the results of their research.

The Newspapers' Handbook. The shelves of bookshops are weighed down with 'how to get into print' and 'how to become a published writer' guides. But by far the best of these for the budding journalist is *The Newspapers' Handbook* by Richard Keeble, published in 1994 by Routledge for £12.99. It covers all aspects of writing for the press, and every aspiring investigative journalist should have access to a copy.

Media Manuals Series. A close second to *The Newspapers' Handbook* comes the Media Manuals Series from Focal Press – an imprint of Butterworth–Heinemann. The series includes *Practical Newspaper Reporting* by Geoffrey Harris and David Spark. The second edition, which has been revised by F. W. Hodgson, offers a detailed guide to all aspects of the reporter's job and is an ideal career introduction for the young journalist. It also suggests fresh approaches to news production while indicating the right and wrong ways of handling news. Also in the series is *Modern Newspaper Practice* by F. W. Hodgson which expands on basic news-gathering techniques.

The Media Guide. Another useful resource on the media for the serious researcher with journalistic ambitions is this paperback by Steve Peak published by Fourth Estate for the *Guardian*. It is packed with essential information including telephone numbers, addresses and contact points for just about every official organization and government department in the country. It also has sections on all of the nation's media and is a unique contact and research directory.

How to get Publicity for Free. This title, written by David Northmore and published by Bloomsbury in 1993, is a beginner's guide to using the press and broadcasting media to gain publicity – mainly for pressure groups and political activists. It provides a step-by-step guide to a few simple techniques on gaining thousands of pounds worth of publicity for a few pence.

Hollis Press and Public Relations Manual. This comprises around 1,500 pages of information on the press and public relations business, including news contacts in commercial, industrial, consumer, professional, financial and corporate sectors; official and public information sources; public relations consultancies (including a region-by-region guide); and reference and research sources;

services and supplies. The manual also has a directory of 'parliamentary consultants', such as the commercial organizations that provide a professional lobbying service in parliament and which hit the headlines several times in the mid 1990s.

Advertisers' Annual. This annual is the main reference book on the advertising and allied industries. It contains detailed information on over 2800 advertising agencies, public relations companies, sales promotions consultants, sponsorship consultants and recruitment agencies in the field. It lists several thousand corporate advertisers and their respective agencies; and provides information on the advertising sales departments in newspapers, periodicals, television, radio, cinema, transport advertising and outdoor poster companies, and also thousands of firms servicing the marketing and advertising industries, such as artists, designers, copywriters, conference organizers, desk-top publishers, research services and allied service providers.

The Advertising Handbook. This book by Sean Brierley of *Marketing Week* magazine is a detailed study of the competitive practices in advertising, including the conventions that govern the industry and those who work in it. It also covers the agency structures, advertiser – agency relationships and the regulation of the industry, such as codes of practice.

BRAD. *BRAD* stands for British Rate and Data and, on a monthly basis, this directory provides a range of technical information on advertising rates for newspapers, trade journals, consumer publications and the independent broadcast sector. *BRAD* is a particularly useful source of information for calculating the economics of a particular publication or broadcasting organization, and of those who advertise in them.

Blue Book of British Broadcasting. This is the main directory of the BBC and independent broadcasting organizations and groups in the UK. It has sections on BBC news and current affairs; BBC television; BBC radio; BBC educational broadcasting; BBC regional broadcasting including local radio; the Independent Television Commission and Radio Authority; independent television companies; commercial radio; and cable and satellite broadcasters. The *Blue Book* outlines the services provided by the broadcasting companies and their programme commissioners, and includes a *Who's*

Who of directors and senior executive personnel.

The BFI Film and Television Handbook. This is an annual publication that provides a mass of data and other information on the British film and television production industry. It provides a statistical overview of productions and awards – the usual trade showcase – but then gets into such subjects as: the legislation controlling film and television production and transmission; cinemas; distributors; courses; facilities; festivals; funding; international sales organizations; press contacts; production starts; specialised goods and services; studios; television companies; video labels; and workshops, etc.

Kemp's International Film and Television Yearbook. This is a specialist trade directory of some 1,700 pages providing details of specialist resources from animation equipment to voice-overs, and includes more detailed information on television production companies, the trade press, and trade and professional associations and societies.

Broadcasting in the United Kingdom – A Guide to Information Sources. The second edition of this widely acclaimed book by Barrie MacDonald is a guide to all sources of information on broadcasting in the UK whether published, manuscript or institutional, and a source of information on the history and structure of UK broadcasting.

Directory of Publishing. This annual directory, published in association with the Publishers' Association and the Federation of European Publishers, is the complete book-trade directory. It has detailed sections on UK and Commonwealth publishing houses, authors' agents, trade and allied associations, agencies and societies, and UK book packagers. Volume 2 covers publishers in 45 countries in continental Europe and highlights those involved in international co-editions. The *Directory of Publishing* contains several cross-referenced indexes that provide speedy access to companies and imprints, names of key personnel, publishers' field of activity, who owns whom, ISBN prefixes, overseas representation, and related technical information.

Keyguide to Information Sources and Online CD-ROM Database Searching. This guide, by John Cox, is a comprehensive and systematic guide to the literature available on CD-ROM, covering everything from specialist journals, reports and theses to directories, bibliographies and industrial trade information.

Law and the Media – An Everyday Guide for Professionals. This guide is by Tom Crone who is a barrister working for Rupert Murdoch's News Group Newspapers Limited, and is an expert on media law. This is a practical reference book in which writers and researchers can quickly find the answers to their day-to-day legal problems, such as libel, copyright, contempt of court and official secrets. The book covers the law relating to all media, including the press, radio, television and advertising.

Newspapers themselves can of course be the most useful source of information on just about any subject. Each year, millions of articles are published in thousands of newspapers and magazines. For a detailed investigative research campaign it may be worthwhile checking the subject in one of the main indexes that cover newspapers and periodicals. These are:

Research Index. This bulky loose-leaf publication provides a detailed index on a range of news stories, primarily on business and financial subjects that have appeared in the national newspapers and in over a hundred specialist trade journals. Headings in the index include government departments, local government authorities, politics, property, security services, trade unions, and newspapers and publishing. Each entry includes the title of the article; the name of the publication in which it appreared together with date of publication and page reference; and the name of the organization or company referred to in the article. This is a cumulative index with bi-weekly updates of around 5000 to 6000 entries per issue.

Humanities Index. This is a very thorough index of a wide range of newspapers and magazine articles covering the arts, economics, history, philosophy, politics and society. A new volume is published each month containing references to the previous month's coverage, and is not to be underestimated for its breadth of coverage despite its off putting title.

Clover Newspaper Index. This index covers a wide range of topics, issues and events reported in the national quality newspapers. The *Index* takes the form of an extremely detailed loose-leaf weekly bulletin and is a very useful starting point for conducting background research on individuals, commercial organizations and official departments.

Back copies of newspapers. Most of the national quality newspapers now produce CD-ROMS of back copies of their newspapers, which are extremely effective for locating historical references to a specific subject. Some major library services will be able to offer this form of data on special readers that allow for the speedy print-out of hard copies of articles from the CD-ROM discs. Otherwise, the researcher has the time-consuming task of locating back copies of newspapers. If the CD-ROM service is not available through your local library service, it may well have back-titles of the quality national press on microfilm from which photocopies can be taken. For more obscure titles it will be necessary to consult the British Library's Newspaper Library at Colindale in north-west London. This library contains some 800,000 volumes and parcels of newspapers and some 250,000 reels of microfilm that occupy around eighteen miles of shelving. Its collection consists mainly of daily and weekly national newspapers and key regional titles, such as the *Western Daily News*, *Yorksire Post*, the *Scotsman* and the like. The library also possesses copies of many London newspapers and journals dating from 1801 to the present. Copies of articles from back-copies stocked by the Newspaper Library can be ordered by post or through a local library service if a specific enough reference can be given for the article required. Telephone enquiries can be made to it on 0171-323 7353; or Fax enquiries to 0171-323 7379. Its address is The British Library Newspaper Library, Colindale Avenue, London, NW9 1XX. The Library is located directly opposite Colindale tube station and is open to the public from Monday to Saturday from 10.00 a.m. to 5.00 p.m. There is no index of the contents of local and most provincial newspapers, but many reference libraries will keep their own files of cuttings on a range of diversified subjects, organizations and individuals relating to their area. The reliability of any such files will vary from library to library, and anyone carrying out investigative research should familiarize themselves thoroughly with the material available.

Chapter eleven

The Political Arena

THE British political system contains a number of honest, decent, respectable and law-abiding characters who have the country's best interests at heart. Unfortunately, though, they are overwhelmingly outnumbered by sleazy, opportunist careerists who use public service as nothing more than a cover for personal advantage and gain. And we all know the identities of some members of both these categories of politician from reading one or two of the quality broadsheet newspapers during 1994 and 1995. That period was the 'cash-for-questions' era – the period in which numerous government ministers and parliamentary aides had to resign for one reason or another, and numerous more had to stand up in the House of Commons and apologize publicly for various misdemeanours. Honour and dignity, it seemed, had gone out of British politics to be replaced by a free-for-all system where some Members of Parliament worked for the highest bidder. And given the lead that the opposition Labour Party had in the opinion polls during that period then it seems as if the British electorate had already delivered its verdict.

But in the meantime there were still some advantages in studying the information that came out of the Palace of Westminster as the individual researcher could often find useful sources of information, and equally useful techniques of obtaining and using inside information that could play a useful part in an investigative research project. The examples contained in Chapter 1 on the National Audit Office and asbestos-related diseases provide an example of the information that can be prised out of government departments and agencies.

Another example of such research is a document put together by academics at the Human Rights Centre at the University of Essex called *EGO-TRIP* – *Extra-governmental Organisations in the United Kingdom and Their Accountability* edited by Stuart Weir and Wendy Hall (Democratic Audit/The Charter 88 Trust, 1994). These researchers painstakingly scrutinized written parliamentary answers tabled by Members of Parliament about the membership of quangos (quasi-autonomous non-governmental organizations). They also drew upon other rare information on quangos in the public domain, such as the annual *Public Bodies* directory which provides some information on the subject.

Over a period of months they pieced together information that showed just how much public money was being handled by quangos with little if any democratic accountability. For example, in Wales, the following major quangos operate (with budgets in brackets where known): Development Board for Rural Wales (£23.6 m); Welsh Development Agency (£165.2 m); 14 Training and Enterprise Councils; 8 Education Business Partnerships; the Cardiff Bay Development Corporation (£48 m); the Welsh Water Authority; the Land Authority for Wales (£6.3 m); 6 Agricultural training boards; 14 NHS trusts (£38 m); 9 district health authorities (£1,307 m); 8 family health authorities (£463 m) 75 GP fundholders; directly-managed hospitals and clinics; Housing for Wales (£187.4 m); Further Education Funding Council (£2 m); Higher Education Funding Council (£0.5); 16 higher education corporations; 26 further education corporations; 7 grant-maintained schools; and 102 registered housing associations.

The research also uncovered the following range of official advisory bodies for the principality: CADW Welsh Historic Monuments Commission; 6 Agricultural Wages Committees; Countryside Council for Wales; Curriculum Council for Wales; National Library of Wales; National Museum of Wales; Royal Commission on Ancient and Historic Monuments in Wales; Sports Council for Wales; Wales Tourist Board; Wales Youth Agency; Welsh National Board for Nursing, Midwifery and Health Visiting; Health Promotion Authority for Wales; Welsh Health Common Service Authority; Advisory Committee for Wales; 6 Agricultural Dwelling House Advisory Committees; Agricultural Advisory Panel for Wales;

Ancient Monuments Board for Wales; Committee for the Welsh Scheme for the Development of Health and Social Research; Hill Farming Advisory Sub-Committee for Wales; Historic Buildings Council for Wales; Housing Management Advisory Panel for Wales; Library and Information Services Council (Wales); Local Government Boundary Commission for Wales; Mental Health Advisory Panel; Place Names Advisory Committee; Urban Investment Grant Appraisal Panel; Welsh Committee for Postgraduate Pharmaceutical Education; Welsh Council for Postgraduate Medical and Dental Education; Welsh Dental Committee; Welsh Industrial Development Advisory Board; Welsh Language Board; Welsh Medical Committee; Welsh Optical Committee; Welsh Pharmaceutical Committee; Welsh Scientific Advisory Committee; Agricultural Tribunal (Wales); Mental Health Review Tribunal for Wales; Rent Assessment Panel, and eight Valuation Tribunals.

However, the people of Wales have no say in the appointment of any of the hundreds or thousands of individuals who sit on these various bodies; they are all appointed by the Secretary of State for Wales. And, in direct defiance of any democratic principles, there are now more 'quangocrats' in Wales than democratically elected members of local government authorities. However, there is nothing new in the expanding role of central government power in this country (although it is unusual to be supplied with such detailed evidence of its expansion). The definitive study on the growth of non-accountable state power that is also not subject to democratic control is a book entitled *The Coercive State – The Decline of Democracy in Britain* by Paddy Hillyard and Janie Percy-Smith (Fontana, 1988). This is a highly critical and detailed study of the subject that should be essential reading for anyone planning to undertake research into central government activity. Despite its age, the book is as relevant today as when it was first published. The Human Rights Centre at Essex University, incidentally, can be contacted at Essex University, Wivenhoe Park, Colchester, Essex, CO4 3SQ.

Members of Parliament

The nation's 650 or so Members of Parliament are fairly well documented – they all have an entry in *Who's Who* – although many of them seem to declare new outside interests every week in the Sunday tabloid press and to various inquiries and commissions into irregularity, illegality and sleaze. Each year parliament publishes a comprehensive *Register of Members' Interests* which is usually available for inspection at main reference libraries. Although this is a thorough register, it is not a compulsory system of registration or in any way regulated by statute. It is a voluntary system, but all MPs agree to comply with registration. The headings for registration include: company directorships; employment or office; trade or profession; clients; financial sponsorships, gifts, etc; overseas visits; payments and gifts from abroad; land and property; and declarable shareholdings. One little ruse that can be pulled on new MPs is this: if the MP is, or was, a councillor at any time since 8 May 1992 – the date that the Local Authorities (Members' Interests) Regulations 1992 came into effect – it is possible to compare the details given on the local authority *statutory* register with the details given on the House of Commons *voluntary* register. For an example of entries on the statutory local authority register see the section on page 24.

Brief background details of Members of Parliament are also contained in a range of other published directories. *The Times Guide to the House of Commons* provides brief biographical details of MPs together with mugshot photographs. It also gives details of their constituency and the voting figures at the last general election. *Vacher's Parliamentary Companion* provides a basic schedule of Members of Parliament, members of the House of Lords, government departments and their ministers, standing and select committees, etc. *Dod's Parliamentary Companion* is an annual directory which publishes photographs and biographical descriptions of all MPs and most members of the House of Lords. Finally, a more quirky publication is *Roth's Parliamentary Profiles* which provides a less formal biographical description of MPs including an outline of their personality-types and oddities; Roth's is clearly the best of the bunch. Another often overlooked source of background information on our elected representatives is provided by past election addresses and leaflets. Reference libraries will often keep a file of such material, and this can occasionally provide information that an MP later on regrets having published.

The Aristocracy

The other half of our parliamentary process is dominated by individuals who are not inconvenienced by having to produce election addresses and leaflets – members of the House of Lords. *Debrett's Peerage and Baronetage* is a comprehensive *Who's Who* of all titled citizens of the United Kingdom and Ireland and the British Royal Family. *Debrett's* includes details of hereditary lords and ladies, life peers and peeresses, law lords, lords spiritual, the baronetage, members of the Royal Family, hereditary peers and peeresses who are minors, aristocratic clubs, a table of general precedence, forms of address of persons with title, and a further mass of information that could not possibly be of the slightest interest or use to anyone.

Parliamentary procedure and documents

Hansard. Everything that is said in the chamber of the House of Commons, or at meetings of parliament's various committees, is recorded in a document called the *House of Commons Official Report Parliamentary Report*, more commonly known as *Hansard*. An edition of *Hansard* is published for each day that parliament sits, and also contains hundreds of parliamentary written questions tabled by Members of Parliament and their subsequent written replies. A single edition of *Hansard* can extend to hundreds of pages, and the only effective way to undertake detailed research using this information is to find a reference library that subscribes to *Hansard*, and spend some time skimming through the detailed data. The Parliamentary Questions and Answers (PQs, as they are known) can often turn up some fascinating material. For example, a Parliamentary Question and Answer entitled 'Brian Patchett' that appears in *Hansard* for 20 December 1994 reads as follows: 'Mr Allason: To ask the Secretary of State for Defence what efforts have been made to trace Corporal Brian Patchett of the Intelligence Corps, formerly based at RAF Gatow. Mr Soames: My Department has no record of any Brian Patchett in the Army. If the Hon. Member wishes to write to my noble Friend the Under-Secretary of State for Defence with more details, he will be happy to look into the matter further.' Most curious, and PQs in *Hansard* are an apparently endless source of leads for journalistic investigations.

House of Commons weekly information bulletin. This is an invaluable source of information about the current progress of parliamentary business, including recent House of Commons business; general notes on legislation; complete list of Public Bills introduced in both Houses of Parliament; proceedings of Private Bills; the progress of Bills; Northern Ireland legislation; Standing Committees; Select Committees; European Communities documents received; the publication of White Papers and Green Papers; recent by-elections and newly-elected MPs; state of the parties in the House of Commons (in statistical terms). Parliament also publishes a glossy weekly magazine, *The House*, while parliament is sitting. This tends to summarize the sort of information better obtained from the *House of Commons Weekly Information Bulletin*, but occasionally publishes interesting features and interviews of parliamentary interest.

Press and television coverage. It is worth remembering that the Houses of Parliament are televised, and both the BBC and independent networks put out specialist parliamentary programmes while parliament it sitting. These are often regional programmes that will concentrate on parliamentarians specific to a television company's own region. Parliamentary proceedings also tend to attract thorough coverage in the quality broadsheet newspapers such as the *Guardian* and the *Independent*.

Public Information Office. This is a free point of contact for the public with its own switchboard on 0171–219 4272. It can answer a range of questions about parliamentary business and individual Members of Parliament over the 'phone, and can also advise on a range of more complex questions and handle postal enquiries at Public Information Office, House of Commons, Westminster, London, SW1A OAA. It also publishes a range of *Factsheets* on a wide range of parliamentary-related issues, and these are normally supplied free of charge.

Lobbying: An Insider's Guide to the Parliamentary Process.
This is an excellent guide to all aspects of the parliamentary process
by the former Labour MP for Battersea, and now life peer, Alf
Dubbs. Although it was first published by Pluto Press in 1988, it is
still up to date in most respects and is the only such guide published
with the public and individual campaigners in mind. It also repro-
duces examples of parliamentary documents which help to
demystify the bizarre language and procedures of this 'Mother of
Parliaments'.

Government documents

Central Government is a particularly secretive area of official
activity which it is difficult for the researcher to challenge. For
example, it is impossible to obtain copies of minutes of Cabinet
Committees or the smaller informal groups operating within the
Prime Minister's office which increasingly determine central government policy. However, the government's own publishing house, Her
Majesty's Stationery Office, publishes a monthly chronological catalogue of all official publications, and this can be useful to check in
the event that a detailed investigation has turned up no other source
of information. The types of document listed in the HMSO *Monthly
Catalogue* are so specialist and so obscure that there is always the
chance that something will slip through the net. All major reference
libraries subscribe to the *Monthly Catalogue*, and HMSO also
publishes an annual catalogue for each category of publication, such
as environment, defence, agriculture, and so on. However, in recent
years the government has published a document entitled *Open
Government – Code of Practice on Access to Government Information*. Although the progressive broadsheet newspapers have been
extremely critical of this code, for a number of good reasons, it is
worth obtaining a free copy (by telephoning 01345–223242) on the
off-chance that in a particular case it may prove useful.

Civil Service Yearbook. This is published annually by
HMSO and is essential reading for all information-freaks and obses-
sives, as well as anyone undertaking a legitimate investigation into
the government sector. This book lists the Royal Household in
considerable detail (every significant post imaginable, including

such gems as 'Clerk of the Cheque and Adjutant' and 'Clerk of the Closet', and the 'Ladies of the Bed Chamber' – of whom there are two, assisted by four 'Women of the Bed Chamber'. It provides details of the parliamentary officers in both the House of Commons and the House of Lords; minister's departments and executive agencies; and an amazing range of organizational charts for the main central government departments. It even includes a list of 'other organisations' ranging from ACAS to the Womens' Royal Voluntary Service. This is a central source of information on central government.

The Statesman's Yearbook. This is an interesting annual publication of statistical and historical information on the States of the world, and includes a thorough personal index of politicians and civil servants. This tome is particularly useful for trying to make sense of the more difficult constitutional aspects of the United Kingdom – such as the government of the Channel Islands and the Isle of Man.

The Diplomatic Service List. This is another HMSO title, and provides details of the staff of British diplomatic and consular posts overseas in 'Commonwealth and Foreign countries', as well as the Commonwealth office in London. It is, however, a little economical with the *actualité* – as they say in governmental circles. For example, it is known that the secret intelligence service, MI6, moved in 1994 to brand spanking-new headquarters at Vauxhall Cross, 85 Albert Embankment, London, SE1 7TP. However, *The Diplomatic Service List* states that this address is simply a 'Permanent Under-Secretary's Department' which is responsible for 'General co-ordination duties and responsibility for liaison with the Cabinet Office and other government departments'. The new telephone number for MI6, should clarification be needed concerning this entry, is 0171–928 5600.

Public Bodies. This is an annual HMSO publication that provides details on some quangos and governmental advisory committees, but not all of them. Given that there are an estimated 9000 individual quangocrats serving on an undisclosed number of quangos and accountable for government expenditure in the region of £40 b per annum, a comprehensive edition of *Public Bodies* would be a hefty tome, but the existing version does provide some curious material. For example, the Department of Health apparently operates an 'Advisory Committee on the Importation of Sexually Explicit Films for Health Purposes' at a cost of £1,000 per year. *Public Bodies* is a useful background research resource.

Government and Industry: A Business Guide to Westminster, Whitehall and Brussels. This huge manual is edited by Lord Bill Rogers and published by Kluwer which is a major publisher in the field of government and parliamentary bodies. This tome covers the legislative process including: parliamentary information and the public; parliamentary privilege and members' interests; ministerial responsibilities; select committees; backbench committees; all-party subject groups; direct contact with civil servants; government departments and other government-sponsored bodies; lobbyists and influencing government policy; the Commission of the European Communities and *Chefs de Cabinet*; members of the European Commission; Directorates-General and Directors-General; the Council of Ministers; the European Parliament; and British MEPs. It also covers local government in the UK.

Political parties and trades unions

Political parties and trade unions tend to attract considerable publicity on a regular enough basis for it to appear that there would be no problem in researching their activities. But this is not necessarily true. Even now the funding of political parties remains something of a mystery. However, one organization that has done a considerable amount of research into this subject is the independent advisory group called the Labour Research Department, which is detailed on page 104. The extreme right in this country is closely monitored by the *Searchlight* magazine at 37b New Cavendish Street, London, W1M 8JR. Telephone 0171–284 4040. A little lateral thinking can be useful when contemplating research on such bodies. For example, the offices of the RMT trade union, formerly the National Union of Railwaymen, in the Euston Road bears a small plaque informing the public that the building is owned and operated by Unity House (Holdings) Limited and is also the registered office of the NUR Employers Superannuation Fund Trustees Limited. So, back to Companies House. And trade unions are required to register with the Certification Office for Trade Unions and Employers Associations, 27 Wilton Street, London, SW1X 7AZ. Telephone 0171–210 3735. The register there is open to public inspection. The Department of Employment regularly publishes a *Directory of Employment Associations, Trade Unions and Joint Organisations* that are registered under UK law.

Whistle-blowers

One result of living and working in a society that is shrouded in secrecy is that there comes a stage when some individuals – particularly individual employees – have to 'blow the whistle'. To become a whistle-blower, however, is a very hazardous practice, as it can result in enormous problems at work or even jeapordize the whistle-blower's career. As a result of this dilemma, and in response to the growth in the number of individuals choosing this course of action, a law centre for whistle-blowers was set up in October 1993 to provide a range of services to concerned individuals and, equally, to concerned employers. Public Concern at Work provides training courses, counselling, legal advice, consultancy and research services, and also publishes a range of leaflets and reports. In 1995, for example, Public Concern at Work published reports on whistle-blowing in the local government and defence-procurement sectors. The Public Concern At Work centre can be contacted at Lincoln's Inn House, 42 Kingsway, London, WC2B 6EN. Telephone 0171–404 6609. Fax: 0171–404 6576.

The master of the official secrecy debate, however, has to be the long-suffering Campaign for Freedom of Information which has undertaken a considerable range of research into official secrecy in the area of central government. Although it is only a small under-resourced organization, it can provide invaluable advice to an individual struggling against the full might of the state bureaucracy. It is located at 88 Old Street, London, EC1V 9AR. Telephone 0171–253 2445.

Chapter twelve

International Research

INTERNATIONAL research is likely to be the most lengthy, expensive and time-consuming work to confront anyone undertaking investigative journalism or research. However, it is possible that there may be an intermediary or other agency that can supply much of the information that is being sought. For example, one UK Member of Parliament tabled a parliamentary question about some aspects of Britain's contribution to NATO's military operations. The appropriate British government minister refused to answer the question for 'security reasons'. So the MP placed a call with a friend who is a US senator in Washington DC. A few hours later the senator faxed the information to the MP in Westminster, as the American politician was able to obtain that information from the Senate Library although the MP was unable to obtain the same information from the House of Commons Library.

Not all of us will be that lucky, although we should not underestimate the significance and quantity of information that can be obtained through other governments. The Campaign for Freedom of Information (details on page 197) is a past master at obtaining information on the British government from the United States authorities.

Press coverage. An individual researcher should start a piece of research with the assumption that somebody somewhere else has already done it, or is in a position to do it. A useful starting point would be to call an overseas bureau of a newspaper or magazine that operates in the UK to obtain some advice as to the type of publication that can be researched on the subject. For example, in the case of the United States of America, there are London bureaux for the following American media organisations: *The Washington Post, New York Times, Los Angeles Times, Chicago Tribune, Philadelphia Enquirer, Time Magazine, ABC News, CBS News,* and so on. Start your enquiries close to home, and then spread out from there. It should be remembered that one volume of the *Benn's Media Directory* (page 181) covers overseas media titles and broacasters. A more detailed reference work on foreign newspapers and magazines stocked in British libraries is the *British Union Catalogue of Periodicals,* and another is *Ulrich's International Periodicals Directory.* Another possibility, of course is to call the London embassy of the country being researched to see if they have any form of public or business library service, and how to use such a library.

Business directories. Well-stocked business libraries, such as Westminster Central Reference Library, the City Business Library, the British Library Business Information Service and most main county libraries around the country, stock a range of business information directories for the main industrialized nations. These are likely to contain little more than basic information, such as goods and services provided, address and telephone number, and such like – much like the information contained in Yellow Pages. One possible domestic source of more technical business information, however, would be trade bodies in this country. For example, if your enquiry is about the workings of the non-ferrous metals industry in Brazil, then the British Non-Ferrous Metals Federation might just be the body for you (it's listed in the London commercial telephone directories and could well house a specialist library).

The European Union. The main source of information about matters relating to the European Union will presumably be a Member of the European Parliament: everybody has one. Given that they have little legislative or executive function, and also given that most people would not know who their MEP is, they should be very keen to assist a constituent who approaches them for information. MEPs can be contacted through the London office of the European Parliament at 2 Queen Anne's Gate, London, SW1H 9AA. Telephone 0171–222 0411. That address will also have a library of European directives, documents relating to the proceedings of the European Parliament and other detailed data: it is advisable to telephone first for an appointment.

The United Nations. The United Nations publishes a wide range of information on international issues relating to the work of its own agencies including the World Health Organization, United Nation's Childrens Fund, the Food and Agriculture Organization of the United Nations, the International Bank for Reconstruction and Development, and so on. The United Nations Association of Great Britain and Northern Ireland exists to support and promote the work of the UN, and has a London office at 3 Whitehall Court, London, SW1A 2EL. Telephone: 0171–930 2931.

Article 19. This is a London-based international human rights organization that fights for the implementation of Article 19 of the Universal Declaration of Human Rights, which reads: '*Everyone has the right to freedom of opinion and expression: this right includes freedom to hold opinions without interference and to seek, receive and impart information and ideas through any media regardless of frontiers*'. This organization is of particular interest to writers and journalists and has a worldwide remit. It is based at 90 Borough High Street, London, SE1 1NL. Telephone 0171–278 9292.

Index on Censorship. This body works on a broad anti-censorship policy around the world and campaigns for individual writers and others who are being censorsed. They publish a regular journal called *Index on Censorship*, and are based at 32 Queen Victoria Street, London, EC4N 4SS. Telephone 0171–329 6434.

Interights. This charity is an international law centre for the protection of human rights, and can assist with pursuing cases through to the international courts for human rights. It publishes a range of reports and briefs on related subjects and cases, and can be contacted at 5 Cromer Street, London, WC1H 8LS. Telephone: 0171–278 3230.

Liberty. Liberty is the National Council for Civil Liberties and has been campaigning for civil liberties in the United Kingdom for more than 60 years. It often takes up freedom of information and secrecy issues, and works closely with other organizations on campaigns and cases. It is based at 21 Tabard Street, London, SE1 4LA. Telephone 0171–403 3888.

Charter 88. This campaigns for constitutional reform that will bring the United Kingdom in line with other civilized countries.

They are at 3 Pine Street, London, EC1R OJH. Telephone: 0171–833 1988.

Amnesty International. This is an internationally renowned pressure group campaigning for the release of political prisoners around the world. It was set up in the early 1960s by a British lawyer called Peter Benenson who had become aware of a handful of cases of political prisoners languishing in a few far-flung prisons. It now has thousands of campaigning activists around the world. The organization was born when Peter Benenson wrote a feature article on the subject in the *Observer*'s Review section – proof that the pen is indeed mightier than the sword. Amnesty International's British Section is at 99 Rosebury Avenue, London, EC1 4RE. Telephone 0171–814 6200. Its international secretariat, which co-ordinates policy across the globe, is at 1 Easton Street, London, WC1X ODJ. Telephone 0171–413 5500.

Centre for Investigative Journalism – A Memorandum of Proposal

Introduction

THE case for a proposed Centre for Investigative Journalism can be stated with relative ease: in the absence of expressed constitutional rights in this country, such as a Bill of Rights or a Freedom of Information Act, the press and broadcast media become the key public watchdogs of the activities and misdemeanours of the State and its agencies – including government departments, local government authorities, quangos, etc – and of such bodies as financial institutions, charities, voluntary organizations and, potentially, any body or institution in our society that possesses and wields power.

However, in the 1990s that task is becoming no easier. In the words of the Guild of British Newspaper Editors: ' . . . the role of the nation's newspapers as public watchdog is being severely blunted by a pervasive, almost institutionalized secrecy in our society.'[1]

This dilemma has not escaped the attention of seasoned practitioners in the field. Following his departure from the *Observer* newspaper in 1990, David Leigh wrote: 'The state of British journalism is the worst that I can remember. When I came into journalism Harold Evans, the *Sunday Times* and the Insight Team were what we all admired. That's all been gone for more than a decade. There's no serious journalism in the *Sunday Times* anymore. It's all consumer tat.'[2]

More recently Stephen Glover, writing in the *Evening Standard*, reported on the difficulties and evident demise of investigative journalism with such observations as: 'Because there is so little proper investigative reporting, it is a safe bet that many abuses of power lie unexamined ... the inescapable fact is that investigative journalism is almost always a little alarming to anyone in power.'[3]

The death of Thames Television's *This Week* programme and Channel Four's *First Tuesday* and the recent announcement that BBC Television is to scrap *That's Life* (a mixed blessing to some) are particularly poignant and topical examples of investigative journalism's continuing demise. Additional evidence includes the decline of Duncan Campbell's routine badgering of the State in the pages of *New Statesman & Society* magazine, and the disappearance of the underground press with an interest in the subject, such as *City Limits*, *The Leveller*, etc.

Unlike the United States of America – which can boast such resources as the Federation of Investigative Reporters and Editors, the *IRE Journal*, the Centre for Investigative Journalism in Oakland, California, and the Freedom of Information Centre at the University of Missouri[4] – this country has no dedicated centre for the development and promotion of investigative journalism and, thus, little prospect of developing and promoting a *culture* of such journalism. This memorandum sets out the potential role for such a centre and can be divided into the following four headings:

1 Information

The key area of work for such a centre would be the publication and dissemination of information for a wide range of readers, and this would form the centre of the campaign to generate a renaissance of investigative journalism and the development of a culture of such journalism. This area covers some four subheadings:

(i) *Investigative Journalism Review newsletter*: A bimonthly or quarterly periodical on the subject would fulfil a number of roles, including: the reviewing of current investigative journalism; in-depth case studies of good (and bad) examples of investigative reporting from the national and provincial press and broadcast media; updates of access to information law; the promotion of the training courses and briefings; policy debate, and so on.

(ii) Briefings: A key service to journalists and other researchers would be the publication of detailed briefings on specific and topical issues, e.g. the Local Government (Access to Information) Act 1985; using the Data Protection Register; researching specific issues such as the arms industry, toxic hazards, financial regulation, or whatever. These can be published on an *ad hoc* basis and marketed on commercial or quasi-commercial terms.

(iii) Publishing agreement: A further objective would be the establishment of an agreement with an appropriate publishing house for an imprint covering investigative journalism and related topics. For example, in 1984 Collins collaborated with the *Sunday Times* Insight team on a book about the DeLorean case.[5]

(iv) Resource centre: It would be appropriate to establish a resource centre of training material, case law, periodicals, books, press cuttings and other resources of use to investigative journalists. This should of course also include information on secondary research sources, such as the British Library Business Information Service and relevant campaigning organizations such as Campaign for Freedom of Information, London Hazards Centre, etc.

2 *Education and training*

Another key function of such a centre would be the training of the next generation of investigative journalists, which would be central to the overall development of the subject per se. Such training could be incorporated into undergraduate and postgraduate courses (both directly and via franchised course units) but consideration should also be given to short courses, professionals' continuing education, the various in-house training courses operated by the major newspaper and periodical publishing houses, plus those operated by such organizations and institutions as the NCTJ and the BBC.

This heading could also include a variety of one-off training seminars on specific issues and even evening classes of the calibre of those offered by Birkbeck College's Centre for Extra-Mural Studies, the City University and the City Literary Institute. The production of training material in the form of distance learning packages could further develop the scope of training courses on investigative journalism. However, such training should not be confined to what is perceived as the 'professional journalist', as there are many others who engage in investigative research and, ultimately, the dissemination of information – activists in Friends of the Earth, Shelter, Liberty and the trade union movement, for example.

3   Research

A Centre for Investigative Journalism might undertake research in a number of areas, including: an historical analysis of the role of investigative journalism and its development – and demise – both in the UK and internationally; a quantitative and qualitative analysis of investigative journalism, both historical and contemporary; and the development of indicators to monitor such journalism on an ongoing basis (assuming, of course, that it is possible to create such indicators). Research along these lines would contribute to the strategic development of the centre and its work.

4   Consultancy and agency services

This aspect of the centre's activity could involve offering a range of research and editorial services on a contract basis, from a one-off research commission to a series of features on a single subject. The agency service could operate on a conventional news agency basis, but dealing primarily with investigative journalism for such clients as, for example, trade unions or voluntary sector organizations.

Funding

For a Centre for Investigative Journalism to be established it would be necessary to plan its funding strategically, and it is anticipated that this would occur in three stages:

(i) *Development funding:* A one-off development grant would be sought in order to commission and publish a feasibility study and strategic plan to expand on the issues outlined here. This should be a detailed document presenting a comprehensive proposal, or a range of options, containing the above elements. This would also be a consultative document containing the views and opinions of a range of individuals and organizations that might broadly support the proposal, and the final publication would serve as a prospectus for the centre.

(ii) *Kick-start funding:* The next stage in funding such a centre would be to obtain kick-start funding to cover the set-up and revenue costs for at least a two-year period during which the centre would be established and become fully operational. At this stage it is envisaged that such funding applications would be submitted to appropriate trusts and foundations, and that more commercial funding strategies would also be developed.

(iii) Ongoing Funding: Once established, the long-term financial objective would be for the centre to be self-supporting through the receipt of grants, fees, subscriptions, affiliations and other income, and there might be scope for the various services outlined here to be structured accordingly.

References

1   Preface of *Officially Secret* (Guild of British Newspaper Editors, 1988).
2   *UK Press Gazette*, 6 May 1991.
3   *Evening Standard*, 19 February 1993.
4   John Ullmann and Steve Honeyman, *The Reporter's Handbook – An Investigator's Guide to Documents and Techniques* (St Martin's Press, New York, 1983).
5   *The DeLorean Tapes*, Ivan Fallon *et al.*, (Collins, 1984).

Appendix two

A Guide to the Data Protection Act 1984

IN May 1981 the British government added its signature to the Council of Europe *Convention for the Protection of Individuals With Regard to Automatic Processing of Personal Data.* Article 12 of this convention states that no computerized data can be passed to any country which has not ratified the convention. Given that all the other European nations had signed the convention, this would have left the UK isolated – particularly in business terms – if it failed to follow suit. It was for this purely pragmatic reason, rather than from any regard for the protection of individual privacy, that a Data Protection Bill was presented by the government to parliament in the early 1980s.

The Data Protection Act 1984 is effectively a freedom of information act that controls and regulates the use to which 'personal data' are put. The Act has three main provisions. First, it requires most 'data users', people and organizations that operate computer systems, to register their use of such data on a public Data Protection Register. This gives the public a very clear view of who holds what personal data on their computer systems. The second effect is that the individual *to whom the data relates* is able to apply to the data user to see their own files and have mistakes or errors corrected. And the third effect of the law is to provide a system of policing and a range of penalties to regulate the use of this type of data and to ensure that it is used only for the purposes for which it is registered on the Data Protection Register. This appendix gives an outline of these three areas.

Details about every individual are held on dozens if not hundreds of computer systems operated by companies, government departments, local government authorities and other official bodies. Most government departments hold personal data on computer systems: the Inland Revenue, Department of Social Security, Home Office, Passport Agency, Driver and Vehicle Licensing Agency, Customs and Excise, Department of Health, etc. Indeed, anyone whose details appear on the Driver and Vehicle Licensing Agency (DVLA) – either as the registered keeper of a vehicle or holder of a driver's licence – will find that their details are automatically transferred to the Police National Computer in Hendon, north London. Each police force in the country then has instant access to this personal information.

In turn, police forces hold a mass of information on many millions of citizens: records of people convicted of offences; intelligence records of people merely *suspected* of committing an offence; details of keyholders of shops, offices, commercial premises; command and control intelligence computers used for the deployment of police resources; intelligence on fraud, terrorism, sexual abuse and other speciailist areas of policing, and so on.

Personal details are also held by banks, building societies, insurance companies, charities, pressure groups, credit card companies, pension funds, employers, political organizations, hospitals, clinics, schools, universities – the list is almost endless. It is also the case that personal details held on computer databases are seen as being valuable information to commercial organizations (as detailed in the example on page 219). The Data Protection Act 1984 seeks to ensure that there is no misuse of all this personal information, and there are eight data protection principles incorporated in the Act.

1 *Data must be obtained fairly and lawfully.* Personal information held by a data user must only be obtained and used according to the Data Protection Act and subsequent legal judgments in both the criminal and civil courts. Data users must not deceive or mislead data subjects; so a company that claims to be carrying out medical research,

but in fact is compiling mailing lists for an insurance company, would be breaking this Data Protection Principle.

2 *Data can only be held for the purposes set out in the data user's entry on the Data Protection Register, and these purposes must be within the law.* This Data Protection Principle will be broken if the data user fails to register all the uses to which the data is to be put, or fails to amend the registration if the uses subsequently change. It is important, therefore, for an investigator to have an up-to-date copy of all the registered entries for the particular data user from the Data Protection Register. These are available free, as outlined on page 212.

3 *Data can only be held for the purposes set out on the Register, and these purposes must be within the law.* The campaigning organization the National Council for Civil Liberties reports that it frequently receives complaints from individuals who find out that information given for one purpose is being used for other unrelated purposes. For example, before the 1984 Act came into effect, it discovered that British Railways made its files of holders of senior citizen's rail cards available to an insurance company. Following the enactment of the Data Protection Act, this would only be legal if British Rail had registered this transfer of data on the Data Protection Register.

4 *Data must be adequate, relevant and not excessive* Another problem is that too much information is collected on individual citizens. For example, a police or social services file that contains speculative information about an individual's behaviour or anticipated behaviour could well be in breach of the Act.

5 *Data must be accurate and up-to-date.* For a data user to comply with this principle, it may be necessary for the data subject to check all their computer files on a periodic basis (say, six monthly) to ensure that out-of-date and irrelevant information is being weeded out.

6 Data should not be kept for longer than necessary for the purpose set out in the Register. Although this principle seems self-explanatory, it does allow for data to be retained for historical or statistical purposes. But, once again, if that is the case then it must be stated on the entry of the Data Protection Register.

7 *Data should be made available to data subjects when they reasonably request it.* Before the Act was introduced it was often the case that the last person able to obtain files held by schools, hospitals, local authorities or government departments was the individual subjects themselves. The Data Protection Act provides a legal right of access to this information: the data subject is entitled to know who is holding what computerized information about them; and they are also able to correct any errors contained in that information

8 *Adequate security measures must be taken to guard against loss of computer files, and their disclosure to people who are not authorized to see them.* With the increasing use of computers and computerized data, it is important to ensure that such information is not obtained by hackers or other eavesdroppers who can use a variety of means of accessing other people's databases. Information must also be protected from abuse by others working for the data user; for example, passwords and other security methods should be introduced to ensure that only authorized personnel are able to gain access to a computer database.

Registration

All data users are required to register under the Data Protection Act 1984 except where the Act specifically allows certain data users not to register. The Act does not give data subjects the right of access to computer files which are:

- manual (i.e. non-computerized files held on paper)
- held solely for domestic or recreational purposes
- for national security (e.g. some M15 records)

- information which the law requires to be made public under other statutes, such as credit reference files under the Consumer Credit Act 1974
- for payroll, pension and accounts
- for mailing lists
- membership lists of clubs
- the prevention and detection of crime or taxation
- for judicial appointments
- documents that have legal privilege
- statistical or research purposes
- prohibited by law from disclosure
- held by financial regulatory bodies
- data incriminating the data user

To register, the prospective data user needs to write to the Office of the Data Protection Registrar, Wycliffe House, Water Lane, Wilmslow, Cheshire, SK9 5AF for a free registration pack which contains a registration form. This is also a useful resource for anyone intending to use the Data Protection Act 1984 as an investigative tool, as it provides a detailed guide to the workings of the Act and of the Data Protection Register. Failure of a data user to register under the Data Protection Act 1984 is a criminal offence which can result in prosecution and conviction in court.

Inspecting the register

The Data Protection Register is a public register that details the categories of information required by every data user who has registered under the Data Protection Act 1984 – but it does not say whether a data user has any information on a specific data subject. When the Act first came into effect in the mid-1980s, the register was produced in microfiche form and supplied to every major reference library in the country. However, since millions of data users have registered under the Act, the register became far too bulky for storage in that way and is now available for inspection only at the head office of the Data Protection Registrar in Cheshire. Obtaining copies of entries on the register, however, is quite straightforward.

First, have an idea of the names of companies or organizations on which you wish to inspect entries from the Register. If dealing with a company that has a number of subsidiaries, it will be worthwhile ordering copies of the Register entries for the parent company and the subsidiaries. This is done by telephoning the Registration Department of the Office of the Data Protection Registrar on Wilmslow (01625) 535711 and giving the names of the data users over the 'phone. The Registration Department will be able to advise you on the number of registrations held on that data user, and can subsequently advise you on the detail of the registration document once it is received. All aspects of this service are free, and will only cost the price of a 'phone call to Wilmslow. Requests for register entries can also be made by post.

But what information might be gleaned from an entry on the Data Protection Register? A demonstration of the value of this information is one of the entries for the Ministry of Defence for its computer that deals with the positive vetting of staff, agents and others, Register entry number G0626166. Purpose 23 of this entry is headed: 'Positive Vetting – Preparation of Reports and General Management'. Under the heading 'Description of Personal Data to be Held' the entry states: 'Employees, trainees, voluntary workers; employees of associated companies or organisations; employees of other organisations; claimants, beneficiaries and payees; account holders; share and stock holders; partners, directors and other senior officers; employers; business or other contacts; advisors, consultants, professional and other experts; members and supporters of a club, society or institution; donors and lenders; offenders and suspected persons; tenants; landlords and owners of property; patients; self-employed persons; unemployed persons; retired persons; students; taxpayers and ratepayers; licence holders; vehicle keepers; elected representatives and other holders of public office; authors, publishers, editors, artists and other creators; immigrants and foreign nationals; relatives, dependants, friends, neighbours, referees, associates and contacts of any of those described above.'

The entry then has a list of 'Classes of Personal Data to be Held' on the subject of positive vetting. The lists reads: 'Financial identifiers; identifiers issued by public bodies; personal details; physical description; habits; personality and character; current marriage or partnership; marital history; details of other family and household members; other social contacts; accommodation or housing;

property and possessions; immigration status; travel and movement details; leisure activities and interests; lifestyle; membership of voluntary and charitable bodies; public offices held; licences and permits held; complaint, incident and accident details; court, tribunal and inquiry proceedings; academic record; qualifications and skills; membership of professional bodies; professional expertise; membership of committees; publications; student records; current employment; recruitment details; termination details; career history; work record; trade union or staff association membership; security details; income, assets and investments; liabilities and outgoings; creditworthiness; loans, mortgages and credits; allowances, benefits and grants; insurance details; pension details; financial transactions; compensation; business activities of the data subject; physical health record; mental health record; disabilities and infirmities; sexual life; racial and ethnic origin; motoring convictions; other convictions; political opinions; political party membership; support for pressure groups; religious beliefs; references to manual files and records.'

The entry then has a section on 'Individuals and Organisations Directly Associated with the Data User' from whom the Ministry of Defence will obtain data. The organizations and departments listed include: 'Inland Revenue; Customs and Excise; Department of Education and Science; Department of Health and Social Security; Department of Employment; Home Office; Ministry of Defence including armed forces; local authority education departments; local authority social security departments; local authority electoral registration, assessment and valuation departments; police forces; the courts; accountants and auditors; credit reference agencies; employment and recruitment agencies; providers of publicly available information including public libraries, press and media; all other civil service departments carrying out PV enquiries; Northern Ireland Civil Service; other organisations to whom security measures are applied, viz Civil Aviation Authority, Post Office, British Telecom, UK Atomic Weapons Authority, and GCHQ Cheltenham.'

Big Brother, it seems, is well and truly in business at the Ministry of Defence. However, this entry from the Data Protection Register gives us an unprecedented insight into the nature of positive vetting investigations; not even Members of Parliament would be able to obtain these details by tabling Parliamentary Questions, as it is ' ... the policy of the government, and has been the policy of successive governments, not to comment on such matters'. So, by inspecting the entries from the Data Protection Register on a target organization, it is possible to gain a detailed insight into their activities that may not be available from any other source.

Obtaining your computer files

To obtain a printout of your own personal file you will need to write to the data user to formally request a copy of the file. Although you can write to any address occupied by the data user to make such a request, it is preferable to write to the address at the top of the Data Protection Register entry which is headed 'Address for the recipt of requests from a data subject for access to the data'. A data user will insist upon a written request for the files as they have to be sure that you are who you say you are. They are under a legal duty to prevent unauthorized access to the data, and part of that duty is to prevent imposters obtaining confidential information by posing as the data subject. The data subject must provide sufficient information to enable the data user to locate the files relating to that individual, and not to confuse one data subject with another who has a similar name. You may also be asked to pay a fee of up to £10 to cover the administrative costs of locating the information. Within 40 days of receiving the data subject's request, the data user has a legal obligation to supply the data – if it exists. Parents are able to apply for information relating to their children, although children are in theory able to apply on their own behalf.

Exam results. The Data Protection Act provides that pupils and students are permitted to inspect the raw marks that apply to examinations. However, as the examining board may be in the process of assessing grades when the request for subject access is made, the law provides that the information must be supplied within five months from the date of application.

Refusal of access. If a data subject is refused access to their computer files, then the individual subject can apply to the County Court or the High Court for an order to see the data – unless the data falls within one of the areas of exemption listed above, or unless in the circumstances it would 'be unreasonable to do so'. For example, if a data user refuses to supply data because it might identify a third party, then the court will have to decide if the refusal is reasonable and therefore within the law.

Correction and deletion. If any information contained in a computer file is wrong, then the data subject can apply to the court to have it corrected or deleted. By *wrong* the Act means incorrect or misleading about a fact, rather than an opinion. If you disagree with an opinion then it can only be deleted or changed if it can be shown that it is based on inaccurate information. If the wrong information has been obtained either from yourself or a third party, then the court may decide that the matter should be settled by the inclusion of a statement of the facts on the computer file.

Compensation. If information held about an individual data subject is wrong, then the data subject may suffer from financial loss and be entitled to compensation for that loss. For example, the National Council for Civil Liberties is aware of individuals who have lost their jobs because inaccurate information has been held on official files. Whether or not the data subject suffers financial loss, inaccurate information can also cause great distress that may result in the court awarding compensation. Another case referred to the NCCL involved a man whose 'previous criminal convictions' were disclosed at court. He was being sentenced for a minor motoring offence when the police announced to the magistrate that he had previous convictions for indecent assault. This information was completely inaccurate as the subject had no previous criminal convictions. If the inaccurate information held by a data user was obtained from the data subject – by making a mistake while filling out a form, for example – then the only remedy will be to have the mistake corrected. The data user can hardly be penalized in court for someone else's mistake. But if the information was obtained from someone else, then the data user is responsible for the error. There are, however, some types of data for which the data subject cannot claim compensation even if it is inaccurate. The data used for domestic purposes, national security data, information already on public registers – such as the electoral register – and information covered by the list of exemptions for unincorporated members clubs, mailing lists, payrolls and accounts. One exception is that the police *can* be sued over inaccurate personal data contained in their files. If a data subject knows that inaccurate information is held about them then the first course of action will be to write to the data user insisting that it be corrected to prevent any further damage. If such a request is refused, then the data subject should take legal advice to see if court action is appropriate.

Disclosure of personal information. As we have seen, the Data Protection Register was set up not only to record what information is held on individuals, but also to state the sources of that information, and the types of individual or organization to whom it is disclosed. So what happens if the data user discloses information in a way not provided for in the registration? For example, in 1984 *Sunday Times* journalists obtained information about a bank account operated by Mark Thatcher, the son of the then Prime Minister. If the Data Protection Act had been in force at the time, Mark Thatcher would not have been able to take the newspaper to court because the disclosure had been authorized by the bank. If, however, the information had found its way to the journalists because of a leak by a member of staff, then the disclosure would not have been authorized by the bank and Mr Thatcher might then have been awarded compensation for the financial loss and the distress that the revelation had caused.

But data users have a defence if they can show that they had taken 'reasonable care' to prevent the loss, destruction or disclosure of information without authority. However, the court can award compensation:

- if the disclosure was not authorized by the data user. (However, if the data subject authorized disclosure but it was in breach of one of the Data Protection Principles, only the Data Protection Registrar can take legal action.)
- unless the disclosure was to someone mentioned in the data user's entry on the Data Protection Register as a person to whom the data might be disclosed.
- unless the disclosure was allowed under one of the exemptions to the Data Protection Act:
    (a) There is no restriction on the disclosure of data which does not need to be registered (see

page 211), such as national security information, information used for word processing or domestic purposes, or which is already in the public domain, such as records at Companies House.

(b) If the data relates to the prevention or detection of crime, the apprehension or prosecution of offenders, or the collection of taxes.

(c) If the disclosure is required by law. For example, a court might make an order for documents relating to a court case to be disclosed.

(d) If the individual who is the subject of the data has agreed to disclosure.

(e) If there is a danger of injury or damage to health, and the disclosure is urgently necessary to prevent such injury or damage.

A data user has a legal defence if he or she can show that reasonable care was taken to prevent the unauthorized disclosure of personal data.

Other legal action. These rights of access to information and to compensation for loss or unauthorized disclosure under the Data Protection Act 1984 are in addition to existing legal rights. For example, if a data subject has an agreement or contract with someone to process data about themselves and the other party breaks the contract by disclosing the information to someone else, then there might be a case for a straightforward claim for breach of contract. Alternatively, the person to whom a data subject entrusts personal information may be careless in disclosing it to someone who has no business to see, in which case there may be a claim for negligence. And if the information was not only inaccurate, but was also published or passed on to someone else, then the data subject may be able to sue for libel or defamation. It is important that anyone who has suffered financially or emotionally because of the misuse of personal computerized information or inaccurate information should take legal advice so that all aspects of the law –

including the Data Protection Act 1984 – can be examined in each particular case.

Case studies

There are a number of cases which demonstrate some of the difficulties and pitfalls in enforcing the Data Protection Act, and which also indicate the 'sharp practices' that some organizations might adopt in order to get around the Act.

A company in the north of England asked its employees to state if they supported the local football team so that it could obtain match tickets at group prices. Quite a nice gesture from an employer, so it seemed. However the company also kept sickness records on its staff – as required by law – and matched the sickness records against the records of their attendance at the local football team's matches. Any member of staff who attended more than one away match whilst on sick leave was sacked. The Data Protection Registrar upheld that this was a breach of the Data Protection Act as the information given about support of the local football team was being used for a different purpose than that for which it was registered.

A market researcher in Kent told a mother that she was working on a research survey for the Department of Education on home computers and their use by children. The mother showed the researcher her child's school reports in good faith, although the researcher was really working for a software publisher who was devising computer programmes that it later hoped to sell to schools through the Department of Education. Processing data lawfully requires that the personal data should only be processed for the purposes stated or implied to an individual. As the reason stated was not true, then the misrepresentation was held to be in breach of the Data Protection Act.

In 1994 the Data Protection Registrar became aware that British insurance companies had set up a centralized database called the Impaired Lives Register. This register contains details of people who have been refused life insurance cover, or provided with life insurance at increased premiums, for health reasons. The Data Protection Registrar conducted an investigation into the practice and established that the insurance companies were using personal data for a purpose other than the principal activities of life insurance administration. It was ruled that applicants for life insurance needed to be made aware of this, and the insurance companies agreed to mention the Impaired Lives Register on life and permanent health insurance proposal forms and leaflets.

One parent complained to the Data Protection Registrar because he had received a postcard from the local health authority about an appointment for the immunization of his child. However, the postcard also contained details of the child's name; date of birth; health authority identifier number; the vaccinations which the child was to receive; the time and date of the appointment; the name and address of the GP concerned; the practice number; the health authority number; and the treatment centre code. The Registrar investigated the matter and the health authority said it would reprogramme its computer to print sealed envelopes containing the information. Several months later the same father received another vaccination appointment postcard detailing the same personal information. This time the Registrar threatened legal action, and the health authority duly set up a new system of ensuring that confidential information was sent in sealed envelopes.

End junk mail misery: this is what one Norfolk man was able to do by using the Data Protection Act. He frequently received unsolicited junk mail from a company with which he had never had any dealings – and he did not want to received its promotional material through the post. So he wrote to the company asking to be deleted from its computer lists. However, the material kept on coming through the post, and so the man contacted the firm's solicitors. They undertook to have his details deleted from the files. But the junk material just kept on a-coming, and so the man complained to the Data Protection Registrar. The company immediately arranged for the details to be removed from its computer, and also arranged for the organization that had originally supplied the information to delete his details from their records.

In 1989 a woman had her handbag stolen, containing a number of credit cards and other official documents. The theft was duly reported to the police. However, the stolen items were used to apply for credit in a store and as a result electrical goods to the value of some £700 were fraudulently obtained by the thieves. When the woman received a bill from the store, the fraud was revealed and this too was reported to the police. The woman also wrote a number of letters to the finance company used by the store, and when she received no further demands for payment she assumed that the matter had been resolved. Four years later the woman's mother – with whom she had been living when the theft and fraud had taken place – had a credit application refused. She checked her credit reference file and found that the fraudulent account opened in 1989 appeared as a default against her daughter's name and, because they shared the same address at the time, against the mother's name too. Both the mother and daughter complained to the Registrar. Although the finance company's records showed that the fraud had been reported, their established procedures were not followed to prevent details from being passed on to the credit reference agencies. The finance company eventually removed the erroneous information from all files, and gave an undertaking that the situation would not arise again.

A man complained to the Registrar that three entries which appeared on what purported to be his criminal record did not relate to him, but probably to another person with a similar name. The police force in question investigated the matter and informed the man's solicitors that the problem had been resolved. However, when he later applied for a Hackney carriage licence through his local council, a search of his criminal record still disclosed these three phantom convictions. A further investigation by the relevant police force revealed that the three convictions had inadvertently been placed on the wrong criminal record, and they were then deleted from the complainant's criminal record and transferred to that on the other individual.

These case studies reveal two main points: first, disputes can often be speedily resolved through the Office of the Data Protection Registrar without the need for legal action. Secondly, they demonstrate the sheer bulk of information that is held on each individual citizen, and the potential harm that can be caused by not ensuring that the information held in such computer files is accurate.

A wide range of leaflets, guides and information packs are available from the Office of the Data Protection Registrar. The basic explanatory leaflet is *If There is a Mistake on a Computer About You*, and a more detailed leaflet, *What is Data Protection?* also contains an order form for obtaining more detailed literature. These include a detailed range of *Guidance Notes* on the register and registration; the Data Protection Principles; individual rights; the exemptions; enforcement and appeals; and a summary for computer bureaux. There are a Small Business Information Pack, a Professional Advisers' Pack, a Student Pack and the Registration Pack mentioned earlier. The Office of the Data Protection Registrar also publishes a hefty tome entitled *The Guidelines* which provides a detailed analysis and commentary on all aspects of the Data Protection Act 1984, and the Registrar also publishes an annual report. This document details all of the disputes, casework and other developments in data protection for the appropriate year, and is a fascinating read for anyone planning to use the Data Protection Act as an investigative tool. All these publications are free, and are available from: The Office of the Data Protection Registrar, Wycliffe House, Water Lane, Wilmslow, Cheshire, SK9 5AF. Telephone (01625) 535777. Fax (01625) 524510.

Bibliography

All the President's Men
Bernstein and Woodward
(Futura, 1974)

An Official Information Act
The Outer Circle Policy Unit, undated)

Beating the System
Bowcott and Hamilton
(Bloomsbury, 1990)

Beneath the City Streets
Peter Laurie
(Granada, 1983)

Books in the Dock
C. H. Rolph
(Andre Deutsch, 1969)

Britain and the Bomb
(*New Statesman*, 1981)

British Intelligence and Covert Action
Bloch and Fitzgerald
(Brandon, 1984)

British Intelligence Services in Action
Kennedy Lindsay
(Dunrod, 1981)

Brotherhood, The
Stephen Knight
(Grafton, 1986)

Challenging the Figures
Christopher Hird
(Pluto, 1983)

Citizen Action – Taking Action in Your Community
Wilson, Andrews and Frankel
(Longman, 1986)

Civil Liberties in Britain
Barry Cox
(Penguin Special, 1975)

Civil Liberties of the Zircon Affair, the
Peter Thornton
(National Council for Civil Liberties, 1987)

Coercive State, the Decline of Democracy in Britain
Hillyard and Percy-Smith
(Fontana, 1988)

Consuming Secrets
National Consumer Council
(Burnett Books, 1982)

Councillors' Rights to Information
Ron Bailey
(Community Rights Project, undated)

Death of a Rose Grower – Who Killed Hilda Murrell?
Graham Smith
(Cecil Woolf, 1985)

Defamation
Duncan and Neill (eds)
(Butterworth, 1993)

DeLorean Tapes – The Evidence
Sunday Times Insight Team
(Collins, 1984)

Democracy Rediscovered
Margaret Simey
(Pluto, 1988)

Dirty Work – The CIA in Western Europe
Agee and Wolf
(Zed, 1978)

Disclosure of Information – A GMW Guide
(GMWU, 1978)

*Disclosure of Information to Trade Unions for
Collective Bargaining Purposes*
(ACAS, 1985)

Doing Business – A Mischief Maker's Handbook
(SPIG/1 in 12 Publications, 1987)

Economic League: The Silent McCarthyism, The
Hollingsworth and Tremayne
(Liberty, 1989)

*Ego-Trip – Extra-Governmental Organisations In The
United Kingdom And their Accountability*
Stuart Weir and Wendy Hall (eds)
(Democratic Audit/The Charter 88 Trust, 1994)

Final Days, The
Woodward and Bernstein
(Coronet, 1976)

Freedom of Information Handbook
David Northmore
(Bloomsbury, 1990)

Freedom of Information Trends in the Information Age
Riley and Relyea (eds)
(Frank Cass, 1983)

Frontiers of Secrecy, The
David Leigh
(Junction Books, 1986)

Gatley on Libel and Slander
Philip Lewis (ed.)
(Sweet and Maxwell, 1981)

Hardship Hotel
Counter Information Services, 1981)

How to Get Publicity for Free
David Northmore
(Bloomsbury, 1993)

Information, Freedom and Censorship
Article 19
(Longman, 1988)

Inside Boss
Gordon Winter
(Penguin, 1981)

Inside the Brotherhood
Martin Short
(Grafton, 1989)

*Inside Your Company – A Shop Steward's Guide to
Company Information*
(TURC Publishing, undated)

Investigative Researcher's Handbook
Stuart Christie
(Refract, undated)

Investigator – A Practical Guide to Private Detection, The
James E. Ackroyd
(Mullen, 1974)

Investigators Handbook
(Community Action, 1977)

Lead Poison
Rick Rogers
(New Statesman, 1982)

Lobbying – An Insider's Guide to the Parliamentary Process
Alf Dubbs
(Pluto Press, 1989)

Local Government Becomes Big Business
John Bennington
(CDP Information & Intelligence Unit, 1976)

*Lost Jobs Wasted Skills – The Impact of Defence Procurement on the
Electronic Sector in London*
(Greater London Trade Union Resource Unit, undated)

Media Law
Robinson and Nichols
(Sage, 1984)

Minding Your Own Business
Marlene Winfield
(Social Audit, 1990)

MPs for Hire – The Secret World of Political Lobbying
Mark Hollingsworth
(Bloomsbury, 1991)

National Security – The Secret State
(Society of Friends, 1990)

NHS – Condition Critical
(Counter Information Services, undated)

Notes for Guidance on Business Names and Business Ownership
(DTI, 1986)

*Nuclear Prospects – A Comment on the Individual,
The State and Nuclear Power*
Flood and Grove-White
(FOE/NCCL, 1976)

Offence of the Realm
Reave and Smith
(CND, 1986)

Offensive Literature
John Sutherland
(Junction Books, 1982)

Official Secret
David Hooper
(Secker and Warburg, 1987)

Officially Secret
Jonathan Aitken
(Weidenfeld and Nicholson, 1971)

Officially Secret
(Guild of British Newspaper Editors, 1988)

On the Perimeter
Caroline Blackwood
(Flamingo, 1984)

On the Record – Surveillance, Computers and Privacy
Duncan Campbell and Steve Connor
(Michael Joseph, 1986)

Out in the Open?
Lucy Hodges
(Writers and Readers, 1981)

Pencourt Files, The
Penrose and Courtier
(Secker and Warburg, 1978)

Phonetappers and the Security State
Duncan Campbell
(New Statesman, 1981)

Political Policing in Wales
Lord Gifford *et al.*
(WCCPL, 1984)

Political Trials in Britain
Peter Hain
(Penguin, 1985)

Politics of Pressure
Malcolm Davies
(BBC, 1985)

Politics of Secrecy, The
James Michael
(Penguin, 1982)

Press and Political Dissent, The
Mark Hollingsworth
(Pluto, 1986)

Pressure – The A–Z of Campaigning in Britain
Des Wilson
(Heinemann, 1984)

Pressure on the Press
Charles Wintour
(Andre Deutsch, 1972)

Privacy: The Information Gatherers
Patricia Hewitt
(NCCL, 1977)

Problems of an Editor
Sir Linton Andrews
(Oxford University Press, 1962)

*Reporters Handbook – An Investigators Guide to
Documents and Techniques, The*
Ullman and Honeyman
(St Martins, New York, 1983)

Research for Writers
Ann Hoffman
(A & C Black, 1986)

Right to Know, The
Clive Ponting
(Sphere, 1985)

Right to Know, The
Francis Williams
(Longmans, 1969)

Secrecy in Britain
Clive Ponting
(Blackwell, 1990)

Secret Society of the Freemasons in Bradford
A. Cowan
(1 in 12 Publications, 1986)

Secrets: On the Ethics of Concealment and Revelation
Sissela Bok
(Oxford University Press, 1984)

Secrets File, The
Des Wilson
(Heinemann, 1984)

Spycatcher
Peter Wright
(William Heinemann, Australia, 1987)

Tracing Missing Persons
Colin D. Rogers
(Manchester University Press, 1986)

Using Company Accounts – LRD Guide
(Labour Research Department, 1990)

Wallraff – The Undesirable Journalist
Günter Wallraff
(Pluto Press, 1978)

War Plan UK – The Truth About Civil Defence in Britain
Duncan Campbell
(Burnett Books, 1982)

Watergate – The Full Inside Story
Sunday Times Insight Team
(Andre Deutsch, 1973)

What Uncle Sam Wants to Know About You – How American Intelligence Works for the Multinationals
(Agee & Hosenball Defence Committee, undated)

Where Have All the Assets Gone?
(Nottingham Alternative Publications, 1979)

Whose File Is It Anyway?
Ruth Cohen
(NCCL, 1982)

Who's Watching You?
Crispin Aubrey
(Penguin, 1981)

Wilson Plot, The
David Leigh
(Heinemann Mandarin, 1989)

Working for Big Mac
(Transnational Information Centre, 1987)

Written in Flames – Naming the Ruling Class
(Hooligan Press, undated)

Index